Monteil
London - July/55

JEAN ANOUILH

Time Remembered

English Version by
PATRICIA MOYES

METHUEN & CO. LTD. LONDON
36 Essex Street, Strand, WC2

This play is fully protected by copyright. All general inquiries should be addressed to DR JAN VAN LOEWEN LTD., *International Copyright Agency, 81/83 Shaftesbury Avenue, London, W.1; all inquiries concerning Professional Performing Rights to* TENNENT PRODUCTIONS LTD, *Globe Theatre, London, W.1, and concerning Amateur Rights to* SAMUEL FRENCH LTD, *26 Southampton Street, London, W.C.2*

First published in 1955

1.1

CATALOGUE NO. 5158/U
PRINTED AND BOUND IN GREAT BRITAIN
BY JARROLD AND SONS LTD, NORWICH

The English version of this play was first presented by TENNENT PRODUCTIONS LTD *at the Lyric Theatre, Hammersmith, on December 2nd, 1954, with the following cast*:

AMANDA, *a milliner*	MARY URE
THE DUCHESS OF PONT-AU-BRONC	MARGARET RUTHERFORD
PRINCE ALBERT TROUBISCOI	PAUL SCOFIELD
LORD HECTOR	RICHARD GOOLDEN
THEOPHILUS, *a butler*	STRINGER DAVIS
FERDINAND, *a head waiter*	GEOFFREY DUNN
THE TAXI-DRIVER } THE GHILLY	NORMAN BIRD
THE ICE-CREAM MAN } THE LANDLORD	HUGH PRYSE
THE CLOAKROOM ATTENDANT	AITHNA GOVER
FOOTMEN, WAITERS AND GIPSIES	CATHERINE COULTON DENNIS CHINNERY PAUL ANSTEE TRISTAM BUTT

The play directed by WILLIAM CHAPPELL. *Scenery and costumes by* PETER RICE. *Incidental music by* LESLIE BRIDGEWATER.

Act 1. Scene 1. The Duchess's Drawing Room.
Scene 2. A Clearing in the Park.

Act 2. The Duchess's Drawing Room.

Act 3. Scene 1. The Blue Danube Nightclub.
Scene 2. Outside the Chime of Bells.

ACT ONE

A drawing room of stupefying elegance. In the midst of the splendour sits a young girl, AMANDA, *with a little cardboard suitcase at her feet. She yawns, fidgets, then finally gets up and begins to examine a Venetian ebony figure of a negro, who proffers his tray of glass fruit ingratiatingly from a marble pedestal. Suddenly she starts guiltily as the door opens, and a little old lady enters with immense dignity, preceded by her lorgnette. It is the* DUCHESS. *She pauses before the negro, adjusts his position to her satisfaction, and then bears down upon* AMANDA.

DUCHESS. So, you've arrived, have you?
AMANDA. Yes, madame ... I think so.
DUCHESS. Stand up straight, child. Chest over toes.

    AMANDA, *bewildered, straightens her back.*

(*Severe.*) How do you contrive to be so absurdly small?
AMANDA. I don't know, madame. I do my best....
DUCHESS. Not good enough. You must make a serious effort.

    AMANDA *looks at her.*

My child, I am sixty. I have improved upon nature all my life, and intend to go on doing so.

    She extends her foot, showing that she is wearing elegant high-heeled shoes.

You must wear shoes, child, shoes ... not plimsolls

like an all-in wrestler. How tall do you think I am in bare feet?

AMANDA. About five foot two, I should say, madame.

DUCHESS (*annoyed*). Not a bad guess. I am five foot one and three-quarters. However, it is of no consequence, as you will never see me in bare feet. I am glad to say nobody has ever seen me in bare feet, except the dear duke, of course. But he was as blind as a bat.

She goes up to AMANDA.

(*Severe.*) And what have you got there?

AMANDA (*taken aback*). Gloves, madame.

DUCHESS (*with a disapproving snort*). Give them to the cat!

AMANDA. The cat?

DUCHESS. I spoke metaphorically. The cat would be horrified. I have a profound aversion to green, which is shared by my Siamese kitten. The sensitive little creature would sooner be made into a meat pie than sit on a green cushion. I may say that she has never seen a green cushion. There is not one single green object in this house—except for your gloves.

She throws them in the fire. AMANDA *cannot suppress a cry of protest.*

AMANDA. Madame! I paid a lot for those gloves!

DUCHESS. You were swindled.

She takes AMANDA'S *hand.*

Good. You have pretty hands. As I thought. They may be accustomed to making hats, but they have a certain air about them. In any case, who hasn't had to make hats these days? I haven't, of course. But then I belong to a different world altogether. Now, I trust that my telegram explained quite clearly why I want you here.

AMANDA. I gathered you had a situation here in the household, madame.

DUCHESS. A situation ... what a delicious expression. The child is quite enchanting.

She thrusts her face to within an inch of AMANDA'S *and repeats:*

Enchanting.

Without taking her eyes off AMANDA, *she adds:*

Is she not, Gaston?

Since there is nobody else in the room, AMANDA *looks round in some surprise.*

I was talking to the duke. He died in 1923, but I have never been able to break myself of the habit of talking to him.

She studies AMANDA *again, then sits down beside her.*

Enchanting.

Suddenly she adopts a coaxing tone, as though speaking to a pampered lap-dog.

And is the little girl pleased to have found a situation then?

AMANDA. Oh, yes, madame. You see, two days ago—I don't mind telling you, because they gave me an excellent reference—but two days ago I lost my job at Madame Rensada's, and——

DUCHESS. I know all about that, dear. I arranged it.

AMANDA (*jumping up in angry astonishment*). You did! Well, of all the cheek!

The DUCHESS *laughs delightedly and sweeps out of the room, saying:*

DUCHESS. Cheek! Cheek, she says! Gaston, didn't I tell you she was adorable ... ?

She has gone. AMANDA *sits down again abruptly. She grasps her little suitcase and looks desperately around, on the verge of tears. A* BUTLER *comes in and bows to her elaborately.*

BUTLER. Her Grace the Duchess wishes me to enquire whether it will be convenient for mademoiselle to partake of a cold collation while awaiting Her Grace's return.

AMANDA. I'm not hungry, thank you.

BUTLER. I beg mademoiselle's pardon, but my enquiry was merely rhetorical. Her Grace has given orders that the cold collation will be served. (*He claps his hands.*)

To the accompaniment of lilting music, a procession of FOOTMEN *stream into the room, bearing dish after elaborate dish amidst a dazzling welter of silver, cut-glass and gleaming napery.* AMANDA *is confronted by a display of cakes, fruits and sweetmeats extravagant enough to daunt the staunchest appetite.*

1ST FOOTMAN. Smoked salmon, mademoiselle?
2ND FOOTMAN. Chicken in aspic?
3RD FOOTMAN. A little lobster?
4TH FOOTMAN. Pâté de fois gras?
1ST FOOTMAN. Iced melon?
2ND FOOTMAN. A peach?
3RD FOOTMAN. An éclair?
4TH FOOTMAN. A tangerine?
1ST FOOTMAN. Chocolate gateau?
2ND FOOTMAN. Wild strawberries and cream?
3RD FOOTMAN. Lemon soufflé?

AMANDA (*angry*). Stop! Please stop! Honestly, I'm not hungry. I'll just have a tangerine. . . .

She takes a tangerine and begins to peel it. The DUCHESS *returns like a whirlwind, followed by* LORD HECTOR, *a tall, thin and tweedy individual redolent of the countryside and its pursuits. The* DUCHESS *bears down upon* AMANDA, *snatches the tangerine away from her, and throws it into the fire.*

DUCHESS. No tangerines, no oranges or lemons. They make you thin, and you cannot afford to lose a single ounce. Now, look at her, Hector. Would she not be quite striking...

HECTOR. Striking....

DUCHESS. ...if we could fill her out a little?

HECTOR, *who has placed a monocle in his eye the better to study* AMANDA, *has no time to reply. The* DUCHESS *sweeps on relentlessly.*

Eggs and pastry, pastry and eggs. (*Calls.*) Theophilus!

The BUTLER *materializes discreetly.*

BUTLER. Your Grace?

DUCHESS. Remove all this paraphernalia and bring the young lady an egg.

AMANDA *jumps up, pale but determined.*

AMANDA. No, madame!

DUCHESS (*turning to her, astounded*). Did I understand you to say "No"? Explain yourself, miss.

AMANDA (*desperately bold*). I'm not hungry and I don't like eggs!

DUCHESS (*to* HECTOR). I told you so. Adorable.

She turns and sweeps out, followed by HECTOR, *who echoes:*

HECTOR. Adorable.

They have gone. AMANDA *can stand no more. She grabs her suitcase, and seems on the point of either smashing something or else bursting into tears. She shouts at the* FOOTMEN *who have arrived to take away the dishes.*

AMANDA. What's happening! Why won't anybody tell me? Why was I brought here?

BUTLER (*as he goes, bringing up the rear of the procession of* FOOTMEN). Mademoiselle must excuse us, but these matters are not confided to the domestic staff. To obtain a reply, mademoiselle must address herself directly to Her Grace—or, as a last resort, to Lord Hector.

He goes. AMANDA, *left alone, throws her case down on the ground and stamps her foot in fury.*

AMANDA. Bother, bother, bother, bother!

DUCHESS (*coming in by another door*). What a hideously inelegant word! Say "Confound it", my dear. That is a fine old full-blooded oath which you can be proud to utter. Bother is not only insipid; it is also ugly.

She sits down, and addresses AMANDA *in a sophisticated drawl.*

I must apologize, my dear, for keeping you here so long—you must be simply *dying* to see your room and have a little rest after your journey—but the fact is that there is a certain person whom I am particularly anxious should not see you, and he is due back from his walk at any moment. It might jeopardize all my plans should you meet him just now.

AMANDA (*sitting down and making an effort to clarify the situation*). I received a telegram from you this morning, madame, saying that you might have a job for me—but I am beginning to think that I must have misunderstood it.

DUCHESS. I am quite convinced that you misunderstood it, child.

AMANDA. I thought so. You see, I'm a milliner, madame. I only know about making hats——

DUCHESS. And you have deduced that I am not the type of woman who has her hats remodelled at home? A good point.

AMANDA. Well, I'd rather tell you straight out, madame, that if the vacancy is for a housemaid, or even a lady's maid... I... well, I'm a skilled worker, madame, and even though it has put me in an awkward position, losing my job at Madame Rensada's, still I'm determined to carry on with my profession.

DUCHESS. You were quite right, Gaston. The girl has spirit.

She gets up and goes to the door, saying to AMANDA *as she passes:*

Another good point!

AMANDA (*jumping up*). No, madame! This time I'm not going to let you go!

DUCHESS. Not let me go? Did you hear that, Gaston? We are to be prisoners in our own home—just as we were under Francis the First.

AMANDA (*a little taken aback*). Francis the First?

DUCHESS. Yes, we were confined to our estates after an abortive attempt to seize power. Apparently we died of boredom.

AMANDA. I promise you, madame, I have no intention of keeping you prisoner. But I arrived here on the 2.17 train, and it's nearly five o'clock now, and the last train back to Paris tonight is the 6.19. If I'm not going to be of any use to you here, I really must catch it.

DUCHESS. No, child, you will not travel by that train.

AMANDA. Why not, madame?

DUCHESS. Because it is not running.

AMANDA. But I looked it up in the timetable!

DUCHESS. I have no doubt that it appears in the timetable. Nevertheless, it is not running—as from yesterday.

AMANDA (*to whom anything seems possible by now*). You stopped it running so that I couldn't get away. Didn't you?

DUCHESS. A hundred years ago, my dear, I would most certainly have done so. No, it was not I who cancelled the train. (*Darkly*.) It was the Freemasons.

She sits down.

They realized, you see, how useful that train was to people visiting this house. We've opened it to the public, you know. Twice a week, ten till six, fifty francs admission. And very nicely we were doing—picture postcards for sale, cups of coffee on the terrace, a tour of the dungeons extra—oh, yes, I move with the times. I realize the value of publicity. And then—out of a blue sky, before I could lift a finger—(*she snaps her fingers*)—they cancelled my train. Just like that. Ah, but I'm too clever for them. Do you know what I'm going to do? (*In a confidential whisper*.) Motor coaches! What do you think of that?

On this triumphant note, she gets up to go. AMANDA, *at the end of her tether, follows her tearfully.*

AMANDA. But I don't understand, madame. I don't know what you're taking about—dungeons and trains and Freemasons. I've been waiting for over two hours and I didn't even have time for any lunch before I left home——

DUCHESS. No lunch? No lunch? What can have happened to that egg? I will go and investigate.

She makes as if to go again. AMANDA *raises her voice in a wail of desperation.*

AMANDA. Oh, madame, please, please don't go away again without explaining things to me, or I'll go mad!

The DUCHESS *stops in the doorway.*

DUCHESS (*serious*). You are cleverer than you look, child. I will make a confession to you. I am not sixty. I am sixty-seven. I have survived the birth of the aeroplane, the death of the corset, short hair and two World Wars. So if I say that I'm an old woman who has seen many bizarre and exciting things in her time, you will agree with me, won't you?

AMANDA (*at a loss*). Yes, madame. . . .

DUCHESS. Well, then, you must take my word for it that the reason I have been popping in and out of this room like a jack-in-the-box for the last ten minutes is simply that I cannot summon up the courage to tell you the truth of why I made you come here.

She goes out, leaving AMANDA *more dumbfounded than ever.* AMANDA *picks up her case, half tearful, half angry, and announces almost hysterically to the empty room:*

AMANDA. Mad! They're all stark staring mad! I'll . . . I'll *walk* back to Paris!

She opens the french window, looks round anxiously to see if she is observed, and then runs out into the garden. The orchestra strikes a mysterious chord. The stage is empty for a moment. Then the DUCHESS *comes in, followed by* HECTOR.

DUCHESS. Hector! Hector, where is she? I have a most curious presentiment——

HECTOR (*looking stupidly round the empty room*). For once your presentiment seems to be correct. She's evaporated.

DUCHESS. She's what?

HECTOR. She's gone.

DUCHESS. Well, obviously. Hector! If she meets him in the park, we are lost! Hurry! Hurry!

They rush out into the garden. The lights dim. The music swells up under a chorus of birdsong. When the lights go up again, we are in a clearing in the park. It is wild and overgrown. There is a small obelisk surrounded by a circular stone bench. At one side of the scene, pulled up near a large tree, stands an ancient taxi. Two legs stick out from under it. A closer inspection reveals that this is a mere caricature of a taxi—filthy and antiquated, and overgrown with ivy and honeysuckle. A cock crows from the vantage point of its roof. Not far away stands an ice-cream cart displaying its gaudy pictorial representations of strawberry and vanilla cones and bars. Two legs are also visible under the cart. AMANDA *runs in, carrying her suitcase. When she sees the taxi, she stops, and exclaims joyfully:*

AMANDA. Oh, thank heavens! A taxi!

She looks round, sees no one, and then notices the legs.

Oh . . . excuse me . . .
A VOICE. Who are you talking to?
AMANDA. I . . . I don't know . . . are these your legs?

A benevolent OLD MAN *appears from behind the ice-cream cart. He adjusts his spectacles, and says:*

ICE-CREAM MAN. Which legs?

AMANDA, *mute with embarrassment, indicates the legs which protrude from under the taxi.*

(*Simply.*) No. Those aren't mine.

He disappears behind his cart again, newspaper in hand.

AMANDA (*as he goes*). Oh, sir . . . please. . . .

He reappears.

Am I still in the park? I've been walking for ever so long.

10

ICE-CREAM MAN (*lugubrious*). Yes, miss. You can walk as long as you like and you'll still be in the park.

A mocking-bird's song shrills out as though to taunt AMANDA. *Suddenly she snatches up her case and runs to the taxi.*

AMANDA. Taxi! Taxi! Driver, are you free?

At these words, the DRIVER *emerges from under his cab, furious.*

DRIVER. Of course I am free. Am I not a Socialist?

AMANDA. Oh, thank goodness, I am saved.

She opens the door of the taxi and jumps in, crying:

Take me to the railway station, please! As fast as you can!

The DRIVER *watches her get into the taxi with mingled astonishment and amusement. She emerges almost immediately from the door on the other side.*

AMANDA. Driver!
DRIVER. Yes?
AMANDA (*angry*). There are rabbits in your taxi!
DRIVER. Of course there are rabbits in my taxi!

He grows very angry.

So now I'm not allowed to keep rabbits, is that it? Eh? Have I or have I not got a right to keep rabbits if I want to?

AMANDA (*retreating a step*). Of course you have a right to keep rabbits....

DRIVER (*advancing angrily*). Am I a human being or am I not? I'm only asking. Getting at me just because they pay me thirty thousand francs a month for doing nothing? Well, I'm not denying it, am I? That has absolutely nothing to do with it. Anyway, I always said I'd never be a private chauffeur... that's what they call me. Huh! Well?

AMANDA (*retreating rapidly*). I assure you I never meant——
DRIVER. All right then.

> AMANDA *takes another step back and trips. She cries out, for by now everything scares her. Then she smiles timidly at the* DRIVER, *as if to excuse her exclamation.*

AMANDA. I'm sorry . . . I'm a bit nervy today. . . .

> *She sees what she has tripped over, and breathes again.*

Oh . . . it's only a bit of ivy. . . .
DRIVER (*calmer*). Of course it's ivy. Any objection?

> *He goes back to his motor.*

It's easy to grow, ivy is. I tried rambler roses once, pruned 'em, watered 'em every day—no good. Wouldn't grow. So now I stick to ivy; it's pretty and it grows quick.
AMANDA. It must be awkward when you want to drive away.
DRIVER. What d'you mean, awkward?
AMANDA. Well . . . the . . . the ivy. . . .

> *By now anything seems possible. She asks with a timid smile:*

AMANDA. Do you . . . take it with you?
DRIVER (*delighted at the idea*). You're a comic, you are. What d'you think the ivy's made of then—elastic?

> *He calls:*

Hey! Giuseppe!

> *The* ICE-CREAM MAN *reappears.*

D'you know what she just said? Asked me if the ivy follows me around! She's a proper scream, she is. Can't you just see me taking it out for a walk every day. (*Calls, as if to a dog.*) Come along, then! (*Whistles.*) There's a good little ivy . . . heel, sir, heel! (*He roars with laughter.*)

AMANDA (*continuing her inspection*). But your taxi can't possibly go at all! There are creepers growing all over it!

DRIVER. What's that? My taxi not go! D'you hear that, Giuseppe? So my taxi won't go, won't it?

He rushes to the taxi, livid, and turns the handle viciously. A hiccough, and the motor starts.

There! Now who says it won't go!

AMANDA. No! No, please! Don't make it move! Not with the ivy! I couldn't bear it! I think I'm going mad . . . everything is absolutely crazy today . . . (*To the* ICE-CREAM MAN.) You . . . are you really an ice-cream man?

ICE-CREAM MAN. 'Course I am, miss.

AMANDA. Well, sell me an ice-cream then. I'm terribly thirsty.

ICE-CREAM MAN. An ice-cream! My dear young lady, it's two years since I last made an ice-cream. I doubt if I could remember how.

AMANDA. Just as I expected. Thank you. You've set my mind at rest. I'm beginning to see a mad sort of sense in all this. I'd only have been worried if you'd *had* an ice-cream to sell—a real, freezing ice-cream. Will you do one more thing for me?

She hands him something.

ICE-CREAM MAN. What's this? A pin? What d'you expect me to do with a pin?

AMANDA. Prick me, please—not too hard, just enough to make sure I'm not dreaming.

ICE-CREAM MAN (*pricking her*). She's a character all right.

DRIVER (*lugubrious*). She's worse than a character. She's looney.

AMANDA. Ow! Thank you. May I have my pin back, please?

She takes the pin, and pricks her own hand, gently, experimentally, as if to confirm her previous opinion that she is awake. Having done so, she suddenly turns to the two men, desperately defiant.

I *am* awake—and alive! D'you hear? I'm alive and when I'm pricked with a pin, I feel it. I've got two legs and two feet, and I can walk on them. I'm not even going to ask you the way to the railway station. I'm going to walk straight ahead and follow my nose till I find the main road. And on the road I'll find a signpost—because in the world I come from—the real world—there are real signposts on the road, pointing to real places! And I'll read it with my own two eyes and then I'll walk to the station, and I'll find the station master—and he'll be a real live station master, made of flesh and blood!

She picks up her case with a sigh which is very close to tears, and adds:

I hope.

As she goes off, she collides with the DUCHESS, *who arrives at a canter, followed by the faithful* HECTOR.

DUCHESS. Oh, thank heaven, we've found her!

She sits heavily on the circular bench.

Oh, child, what a fright you gave me! I nearly died ... and I am prostrate with exhaustion.

AMANDA. Don't try to make me feel sorry for you. What about me? *I*'m exhausted too, and *I* nearly died of fright.

DUCHESS. Fright? What on earth is there for you to be frightened of?

AMANDA. Everything, madame—especially you.

DUCHESS. Me? What an extraordinary notion. D'you hear that, Hector?

AMANDA (*lively*). Yes—you! And the taxi-driver whose taxi is overgrown with ivy, and the ice-cream man who hasn't sold an ice-cream for two years, and this awful park with no way out of it . . . Where am I? What do you want of me? Why did you get me dismissed from Madame Rensada? Why did you entice me out here by promising me a job—what sort of job could I possibly do in this madhouse? I suppose you want a milliner who doesn't make hats! (*Determined.*) Well, I'm not frightened of you any more. Which is the way to the station? I demand that you tell me the way to the station!

DUCHESS. Hector, she is adorable.

HECTOR. Adorable.

> AMANDA, *worn out, sinks on to the bench, crying amidst her sobs:*

AMANDA. Tell me the way to the station!

DUCHESS (*taking her hand*). No, no! You must on no account cry! I appreciate your confusion and your curiosity, child. The moment has come for plain speaking, however painful. I will be brief. I have a nephew, mademoiselle. A nephew whom I idolize above everything else in the world. His name is Albert. The poor boy is the victim of a most strange melancholia, which——

> *She stops.*

The story is so poignant to me that I really cannot bear to repeat it. Hector, you go on.

> HECTOR *stands up, ceremoniously. The* DUCHESS *introduces him in a brisk tone.*

Allow me to present my cousin, Baron Andinet of Andaine.

> HECTOR *bows.* AMANDA *drops a little curtsey.* HECTOR *is about to speak, but the* DUCHESS *forestalls him.*

Lord Hector. He is not to be confused with Lord Jerome, who is first secretary at the consulate in Honolulu, nor with Lord Jasper, the General's son. (*With a gesture.*) Lord Hector.

> HECTOR *bows again, and opens his mouth to speak. Once more he is too late.*

There is very little likelihood of your confusing him with Lord Jasper. He has been dead for some years, poor fellow.

HECTOR. Poor fellow!

DUCHESS. Go on, Hector.

HECTOR. Well, mademoiselle, my cousin, Prince Troubiscoi . . .

DUCHESS. Yes, my sister became a Troubiscoi by her second marriage, the silly girl. The Tsar was visiting Paris at the time—Slavonic charm, I am afraid, quite fatal—however, we've been into all that . . . go on, Hector.

HECTOR. My cousin, Prince Troubiscoi——

DUCHESS. Call him Prince Albert, or she may think you are referring to the other one—that imbecile who married the Englishwoman—Patrick Troubiscoi. (*To* AMANDA, *perfectly naturally.*) You may have met him?

AMANDA. No, madame.

DUCHESS. You amaze me. One meets him absolutely everywhere. Go on, Hector.

HECTOR. Well, mademoiselle, some years ago my cousin, the Prince Albert, visited Dinard, where he met a young woman who——

DUCHESS (*interrupting*). No, no, no! Be quiet, Hector. You manage to invest the story of this exquisite romance with such a flat-footed platitudinous boredom that I prefer to make the sacrifice and tell it myself. Two years ago, mademoiselle, my beloved Albert became deliriously enamoured of a lady of incomparable beauty and impeccable aristocracy... a lady of whom you will certainly have heard. I will tell you her name. Léocadia Gardi.

AMANDA. The ballerina?

DUCHESS. Yes, child. The great and glorious ballerina. The divine Gardi, as they called her. Ah, the exquisite, ethereal grace of that first entry of hers in *Lac des Cygnes*.

She dances a few steps, then stops.

Unhappily I am no dancer. When I was a girl I was as light as thistledown on my feet—but thirty years of waltzing with the dear duke proved too much for my delicate talent... a pity, but there it is. Where was I?

HECTOR. In the *Lac des Cygnes*.

DUCHESS. Oh, yes... Léocadia. Dear Léocadia. You say you knew her well. That will be the greatest help to us.

AMANDA. Oh, no, I didn't know her at all. I just read about her death in the newspapers.

DUCHESS. Alas, yes! You know how she died?

AMANDA. I think they said it was an accident.

DUCHESS. Yes. The poor darling always wore a scarf of immense length; she had a different one for every costume she possessed... very becoming they were, too... they became quite a legend, Léocadia's scarves. As she said good-bye to you, she would fling her scarf around her lovely neck, and knot it in her own inimitable way.... Well, one evening she was leaving the house of some friends after a most interesting discussion on the thirty-two *fouettés*. On the doorstep, saying good-bye, she knotted her scarf with a magnificent, characteristic gesture. (*She demonstrates.*) Alas, she flung her arm too wide...

strangled herself. She let out a single cry—a strangled one, of course—and fell, dead.

She sniffs.

Finish it, Hector. I can't go on.

HECTOR (*who is under the impression that it is already finished, merely repeats*). Dead. . . .

DUCHESS. It was only three days before this tragedy that poor Albert fell in love with her. He has never recovered from those three days. Now do you begin to understand?

AMANDA. No.

DUCHESS. Very well, I will proceed. When he heard the ghastly news, his first thought was to fling himself from his balcony. For more than an hour I held him back by his coat-tails with my own hands. But that was merely a temporary danger. I had to think of the future. I decided that he must travel. We went on a most expensive and enthralling cruise—one and a half times round the world— but all in vain. One hundred and twenty-two days we spent on that peregrination—Albert sitting in his cabin gazing at a photograph of his dear departed, and me sitting in mine gazing at him through the intervening keyhole, to make sure he did not jump overboard. Do you wish me to describe to you in detail the agonies of my long martyrdom?

AMANDA (*who is beginning to be fed up*). No, madame.

DUCHESS. No. You are right. It would be too long and too painful. Suffice it to say that I, the very soul of curiosity, travelled one and a half times round the world with one eye shut and the other glued to a keyhole. Now and then, when we were in harbour, my gipsy nature became too strong for me, and I would snatch a peep through the porthole. Once I caught a glimpse of a turban—that was India. Another time, a pigtail—China, of course. The smoke of a volcano told me we were approaching Italy

... only when we were on French soil once more did I dare to think of myself again.... I found I had lost two stone through worry and anxiety... fortunately however, the lack of exercise had put it on again... we are now in Marseilles. Are you following me, or am I going too fast for you?

AMANDA. No, madame. I'm with you.

DUCHESS. Good. We returned home with all speed—we both needed a rest. At last I seemed to detect a lessening of Albert's grief... but his melancholy was still deep enough to worry me. I set my spies on him, to report on his every movement. I learnt that he spent his days in Dinard, chatting sometimes with a taxi-driver, sometimes with an ice-cream merchant, sometimes with the landlord of a wretched little inn called the Chime of Bells. As for his evenings, he invariably went to a certain Viennese nightclub, sat always at the same table, and was served always by the same waiter. September came... Dinard was deserted.

HECTOR. Always is in September.

DUCHESS. All the cafés closed for the winter—except that one. It remained open, and night after night Albert sat there in solitary state. Soon I discovered that he was financing the place, which otherwise would have been bankrupt long ago—simply for the pleasure of being able to sit at that particular table every night. Frankly, I was baffled. I could not understand—and then, suddenly, I saw the light!

AMANDA (*who is beginning to take an interest in the love story*). Was it there that they first discovered that they loved each other?

DUCHESS (*regarding her admiringly*). Oh, Hector! What a splendid thing it is to have a plebeian soul! The girl has understood instinctively what we, with our intelligence, took months to grasp. Yes, child, you are right. The taxi-driver, the ice-cream man, the Chime of Bells, the gipsy café . . . all of them formed the background of poor Albert's love affair with his divine Léocadia, and every day for three long months he returned to their enchantment, like a man possessed.

AMANDA (*dreamy*). It must be wonderful to love someone as much as all that. . . .

DUCHESS. I dare say. But think of my position. Albert is not only a Troubiscoi, but—far more important—he is an Andinet of Andaine, on his mother's side. Please don't think I am simply a reactionary old fossil—nothing could be farther from the truth. In the first war, I signed on to the nursing reserve without making any stipulation whatsoever about the social status of my patients . . . I felt I must set an example. But all the same . . . all the same . . . you must admit that it is scarcely worth going to the trouble and expense of gaining control of half the kingdom in the reign of Louis the Great, if a mere seven hundred years later one is going to have one's nephew gossiping on street corners with taxi-drivers and ice-cream men. However . . . where was I?

HECTOR. You'd suddenly seen the light.

DUCHESS (*picking up the thread*). Ah, yes. I realized suddenly that these people were merely the souvenirs of dear Albert's great love. Well, I am a collector at heart. I bought the taxi, the ice-cream cart, the park benches upon which they sat . . . these benches were the most difficult of all. . . . I had to go to court over them—but I got them. As for the inn and the Viennese nightclub, I had them rebuilt stone by stone in the park.

AMANDA. It's . . . it's like a fairy story . . .

DUCHESS. Nonsense. It was the least I could do. I confess I am thankful that the poor children did not visit the Eiffel Tower. . . .

AMANDA. How you must love your nephew, madame!

DUCHESS. My dear, I worship him— and so will you, when you meet him. In any case, Albert and I are both stay-at-homes by nature, and so I have arranged that the dear boy shall have his precious souvenirs within easy reach.

AMANDA. But I still don't understand where I fit in, madame. I promise you I've never set eyes on your nephew at any time—let alone during those three fatal days—I can't possibly be one of his souvenirs. I've never set foot in Dinard in my life. Why, when Léocadia Gardi died, I was working for Madame Rensada from nine till six every day. It was my first year, and I didn't have a holiday at all that summer—I can prove it! I had no chance to go to the seaside!

DUCHESS (*to Hector*). Hector, I find her quite delightful.

HECTOR. I must admit she's rather pretty.

DUCHESS. She is far more than just pretty. She has spirit.

HECTOR. That's what I meant.

DUCHESS. Hector, you're pathetic. (*To* AMANDA.) Pay no attention to him, dear. You have spirit. A quality all too rare these days.

AMANDA (*lively*). I am well aware that I have spirit, madame. But I was not aware that my reputation for it had spread all the way down here from the Rue de la Paix. Don't try to tell me that *that's* why you sent for me!

DUCHESS. No, child.

She suddenly seems uneasy.

What time is it? Here we are, chattering away . . . it must be quite late. . . .

She starts to rise.

AMANDA (*desperate, pushing her down again*). No, madame. Sit down and give me a straight answer for once. I don't know what time it is, and I don't care. I've missed my train back anyway, thanks to you. . . .

DUCHESS. Nobody has ever dared to use that tone with me—not even the dear duke!

AMANDA. Well, nobody has ever dared to lure me into the wilds of Brittany by promising me a job, and then refused to tell me what the job is!

DUCHESS (*to* HECTOR). This is painful for us, Hector, but we have asked for it. (*Resolute.*) Hector, we must tell her.

HECTOR (*unenthusiastic*). Yes, we must.

DUCHESS. We must.

A long pause. They stare into the distance, deeply embarrassed.

(*Suddenly.*) Hector.

HECTOR. Yes.

DUCHESS. Are you a man or a mouse?

HECTOR (*without hesitation*). A mouse.

DUCHESS. What?

HECTOR (*pathetic but firm*). A mouse. You're always telling me so.

DUCHESS (*annoyed*). Only in fun, Hector. Of course, you're a man. Tell the girl the truth, before she begins to suspect the worst.

AMANDA. I suspect the worst already, madame.

DUCHESS. My dear child, what you call the worst is the least of your worries. It is far worse than the worst. Go on, Hector. We are waiting.

HECTOR (*after much preliminary clearing of the throat*). Well . . . the fact is . . .

Pause. In a strangled voice:

No, I can't say it! It was your idea, anyway!

DUCHESS. Very well. I will meet you halfway. Let us speak in unison.

HECTOR. In unison?

DUCHESS (*ironic*). Unless you feel up to the descant. We will recite together the speech we prepared this morning.

HECTOR. Word for word?

DUCHESS. Word for word. Watch my hand. One, two, three . . . ready?

HECTOR. Yes, I suppose so.

DUCHESS. Go!

They take a step forward, and begin, together:

DUCHESS AND HECTOR. Mademoiselle . . . or rather . . . dear child, if we may presume so to address you. . . .

They look at each other, and take a breath in unison. Then they continue.

Dear child . . . what we have to say may shock you, coming as it does from such irreproachably respectable lips as ours. . . .

HECTOR'S *voice has trailed off miserably. The* DUCHESS *gives him an admonitory look.*

DUCHESS. Hector, where are you?

HECTOR. It's no good . . . I can't say it . . . not even in unison!

DUCHESS (*sad*). To think that an ancestor of yours once defended a bridge single-handed against the entire Albanian army.

HECTOR (*stung*). That has nothing to do with it! Show me the Albanian army, and I'll defend a bridge against it with pleasure. But this is a different kettle of fish altogether, and I want no part of it.

DUCHESS. Very well. In that case, go away. Since the head of my family turns tail at the first whiff of grapeshot, I shall have to carry the banner alone! Leave us!

Hector goes, his head bowed in shame. The DUCHESS *abandons her belligerent attitude, and draws* AMANDA *to her, speaking more quietly and with less buffoonery than before, a genuine sensitivity shining under the raillery which makes her suddenly warm and human.*

DUCHESS. Well, child. I suppose you think I'm a mad old woman . . . no, no, don't deny it . . . but I do assure you that I'm not. I know perfectly well that you will be offended by what I'm going to say. You will stand up in adorable affronted dignity, clutching your little cardboard suitcase, and slip away through my fingers into the dusk.

She looks at AMANDA, *then goes on:*

And the tragic thing is that if you were my daughter, that is just what I would want you to do . . . and yet . . . my dear . . . no one can overhear us . . . and even you and I are beginning to grow dim to each other, as the violet velvet of the evening falls tactfully between us, until your face is only a glimmer of whiteness in the twilight. . . .

She stops, and dreams a little.

If you were my daughter . . . but I have no daughter. I could never have a child. Was it poor Gaston's fault or mine? I never knew. And when he died it was too late for me to find out. I have no daughter. But I have a nephew. Perhaps it is naughty of me to be so indulgent with him. . . but it is only because I love him too well . . . and in any case, I am extravagant by nature.

A little pause. She looks at AMANDA *again.*

If you were my daughter . . . but there it is. Providence sends us good fortune and bad—burdens we feel we shall never be able to bear, and blessings we forget too soon. Sometimes we have bitter rôles to play, believe me. And here I am, near the final curtain of my life, playing a ridiculously unsuitable part for a woman in my position . . . but you . . . you are so young . . . standing in the wings of your life . . . waiting to make your entrance, tremulous on the brink of adventure . . . it would be so easy for you to come to the rescue of a poor old woman who is at her wit's end.

AMANDA (*a murmur*). I don't understand what you mean, madame.

DUCHESS. I did not intend that you should, my dear. I am only talking to myself—rambling on to spin out the tardy time until the dusk deepens to hide my blushes. How strange it feels to blush. I have not blushed since I was a little girl in a crinoline and frilly pantaloons, made to stand in the corner because I refused to kiss a Field Marshal with a black beard.

Pause. It grows darker.

AMANDA (*a whisper*). It is almost dark now, madame . . .

DUCHESS (*a sudden brisk voice from the gathering gloom*). Tell me then, child—have you had many lovers?

AMANDA (*taken aback*). Lovers?

DUCHESS. Flirtations, I mean. Nothing serious. Snatched kisses in the shrubbery after a croquet party—oh, what am I saying! I simply cannot get my epochs right! I should say, of course, snatched kisses in the darkness of the cinema, or behind the springboard at the lido.

AMANDA *is silent. Pause.*

(*A little weary*). Now I've frightened you. Or even disgusted you. I don't want to know whether you have ever been in love, child. I wouldn't pry into your secret heart. I am simply talking about flirtations.

AMANDA (*soft, after a pause*). Yes, madame. I have had flirtations, but I have never been in love.

DUCHESS. Life is full of delicious surprises, child. One day love will burst upon you out of a clear sky in a sudden golden glory. Until then, you must live as intelligently as you can from day to day, and when your moment of happiness comes . . . seize it with both hands—be greedy —don't waste it, for it will never come again.

Pause.

But I did not mean to speak of love.

Pause.

Albert is a fine, handsome boy—but all his youth and gaiety have been numbed by his sorrow. One day he will take his own life, tomorrow perhaps, perhaps the day after . . . I don't know. But one day he will do it, unless he can find some echo of Léocadia, something more satisfying than the bricks and mortar which sheltered her, or the fools who knew her when she lived, but haven't the wit to conjure up her spirit for him now that she is dead. I am a very influential old woman, even in these democratic days, and ludicrously rich, and yet I cannot lift a finger to save his life . . . and afterwards I shall be alone, and as useless as a pile of dead ashes on a windy day.

AMANDA. How can I help him, madame? I dare not think that you mean . . . well . . . in any case, why me? I'm not very pretty. And even if I was, how could anybody come between him and his memories?

DUCHESS. Nobody could—except you.

AMANDA (*amazed*). Me?

DUCHESS. The first time I saw you in Madame Rensada's

shop, child—I wept. Because, to anyone who knew her as she really was, you are the living image of Léocadia.

Silence. The nightbirds have taken over from the day-time songsters. The park is vibrant with rustling leaves and chasing shadows.

AMANDA (*very soft*). Even so, I'm afraid I can't do it, madame. I may be poor and insignificant, but at least my flirtations have been my own. . . .

DUCHESS (*soft and very sad*). Of course. I beg your pardon.

She gets up slowly. For the first time, we realize what a very old lady she is. Suddenly there is the sound of a bicycle bell. The DUCHESS *trembles.*

Listen! There he is! Oh, let him see you standing beside the obelisk, where he first met her! Let him see you just once—and cry out, be horrified, anything! I swear I will tell him tomorrow that it was a trick I played on him, even though he may hate me for it. It's worth it, if only I can see him stung into feeling again by something alive—by anything except that relentless ghost who is forever beckoning, enticing him to join her in the shadows.

She grasps AMANDA'S *arm.*

I beg you, mademoiselle . . . on my knees. Take pity on me.

She looks at her imploringly then adds quickly:

And you will see him, too. And . . . great heavens, I'm blushing again . . . the third time in sixty years and the second time in ten minutes . . . how gloriously illogical life is. My dear, he is handsome, he is charming. Why shouldn't he be one of your very own flirtations—for a moment?

The bicycle bell sounds again, closer.

AMANDA (*a whisper*). What shall I say to him?
DUCHESS (*embracing her*). Just say, 'Excuse me, can you tell me the way to the sea?'

She disappears into the deep shadows under the trees—just in time. Out of the darkness, the shadow which is the PRINCE *on his bicycle passes close to the shadow which is* AMANDA *standing by the obelisk.*

AMANDA. Excuse me. . . .

The PRINCE *stops, gets off his bicycle, and sees her.*

PRINCE. Yes, mademoiselle?
AMANDA. Can you tell me the way to the sea?
PRINCE. The second turning on the left, mademoiselle.

He bows stiffly and sadly, remounts and cycles off. The bell sounds again, receding into the distance. The DUCHESS *emerges from the shadows. Pause.*

AMANDA (*soft*). He didn't recognize me. . . .
DUCHESS. It is very dark . . . and then he may remember her differently after all this time. (*Pause, then she says, almost shyly.*) The last train has gone, mademoiselle. Won't you change your mind and stay with us tonight?
AMANDA (*after a pause, softly*). Thank you, madame. . . .

The darkness has really closed in now, and the figures of the two women can no longer be distinguished in the gloom. Only the wind can be heard sighing in the tall trees. The curtain falls.

ACT TWO

The DUCHESS'S *Drawing Room. Morning. The* BUTLER *stands there, like a statue. He appears to be waiting for something. The door opens and a man comes in. In dress, deportment and manner, he is as like the* BUTLER *as two peas in a pod. He is the* HEAD WAITER. *The two regard each other with hostility.*

HEAD WAITER. Good morning.
BUTLER. Good morning.

Pause. They look each other up and down. The BUTLER *straightens his bow-tie. In spite of himself, the* HEAD WAITER *does the same.*

May one ask to what we owe the pleasure of your company?
HEAD WAITER. Her Grace requested me to wait upon her here at nine o'clock, in order to discuss certain details relating to the entirely imaginary Viennese nightclub which I run in the park.
BUTLER (*with a tinge of bitterness which he takes pains to conceal*). In that case, won't you take a seat?
HEAD WAITER. I am much obliged to you.

He sits down, stiffly. The BUTLER *makes as if to leave the room, pausing as he goes to adjust the position of the Venetian negro, with an authority calculated to drive home the fact that this is his domain. At the door, however, he changes his mind and comes back.*

29

BUTLER. I wonder if I may have a word in your ear?

HEAD WAITER. You may.

BUTLER. I myself have been in service all my life with high-class families—representing, I flatter myself, all that is best in the upper reaches of society. But I have a brother-in-law who has elected to pursue his profession in the hotel and restaurant side of our calling—for the sake of money. He has been employed at the Waldorf, the Savoy, the Excelsior . . . perhaps you may have heard of these establishments?

HEAD WAITER. I have heard of them.

BUTLER. Now, I must confess that in him, and in his colleagues, I have always detected a certain slackness . . . a tendency towards familiarity, which invariably characterizes those who habitually serve a customer rather than a master.

HEAD WAITER (*inscrutable*). I fear I cannot follow your train of thought.

BUTLER. I will elucidate. I have failed, to my great astonishment, to observe in you any sign of this degeneracy. I understand you used to work in Dinard, in a short-lived establishment which, if I may say so, could not in the nature of things have been . . . shall we say . . . five star.

HEAD WAITER (*pale*). It was an excellent restaurant of its kind . . . excellent . . . but five star, no. Three, say. But not five.

BUTLER. As I thought. So I would like to put a question to you. Did you not spend long years of service in a private household before——

HEAD WAITER (*bowing his head, with a stifled sob*). Yes, you are right. I did . . . before . . . but then one day——

BUTLER (*silencing him with a gesture*). Please. Please. Far be it from me to pry into the reasons for your downfall. I merely wished to verify my contention that a butler who is worthy of the name can always be distinguished by a standard of etiquette which no degradation can eradicate.

HEAD WAITER (*raising his head*). Thank you.

BUTLER (*affable and superior*). Think nothing of it, my dear fellow. You must forgive me if I have twisted the knife in an old wound. The subject will never be mentioned again. (*Formal.*) I will inform Her Grace of your arrival.

He goes. The DUCHESS *enters in a whirl as usual, followed by* HECTOR *and* AMANDA. *The latter is dressed in the flamboyant style which one would associate with Léocadia.*

DUCHESS (*to the* HEAD WAITER). Ah, there you are, Ferdinand.

HEAD WAITER (*rising precipitately*). Good morning, Your Grace.

DUCHESS (*a cry*). Don't say good morning to me yet! Look at this young lady. Study her from every angle! Well, what have you to say to me now?

The HEAD WAITER *looks at* AMANDA, *somewhat bewildered at first, and not understanding what the fuss is about. Then suddenly, realization breaks upon him.*

HEAD WAITER. Great heavens!

The DUCHESS *forgets herself to the point of seizing his hand in her enthusiasm.*

DUCHESS. Thank you! Oh, thank you for that! (*To* AMANDA.) We have succeeded, child. Come and kiss me.

She kisses AMANDA. *Then she turns to the* HEAD WAITER *again.*

Now you may wish me good morning.

HEAD WAITER. Good morning, Your Grace.

DUCHESS (*in her usual, aloof tone*). Good morning, Ferdinand.

She indicates AMANDA.

Well? Is it not truly amazing?

HEAD WAITER. It's . . . it's phantasmagoric, Your Grace.

DUCHESS (*a cry*). Phantasmagoric! The very word I have been searching for since yesterday! Phantasmagoric! That is exactly it. Where did you find it?

HEAD WAITER. What, Your Grace?

DUCHESS. That word! Where did you find it?

HEAD WAITER. I really don't know, Your Grace . . . in a newspaper, I think . . .

DUCHESS. Ah, I never read the newspapers. That accounts for it. All the same, it is the exact word I want. Phantasmagoric. (*She is delighted.*) Phantasmagoric! You are phantasmagoric, child!

AMANDA. I don't much like the sound of it, madame.

DUCHESS. Oh, what a quaint girl it is! Don't worry, child, you may appear phantasmagoric to us, but in reality you are a Greuze. A little living Greuze.

HECTOR. I'd say she has more of the piquant, provocative quality of a Boucher.

DUCHESS. Fiddlesticks. Don't talk nonsense, Hector. She is not at all a Boucher, she is a Greuze. When she smiles, I will grant you a fleeting glimpse—no more— of a Le Nain shepherdess . . . (*To* AMANDA.) Has nobody ever remarked on it before?

AMANDA (*simply*). No, madame. I've never heard of any of those people.

DUCHESS. She is adorable, Hector.

HECTOR. Adorable.

DUCHESS (*to* AMANDA, *as though explaining to an imbecile*

child). They are painters, dear. Great artists who lived long ago, and painted pictures . . . with paint brushes . . .
AMANDA (*a little smile*). Yes, I know what a painter is.
DUCHESS (*off-hand*). I have a couple of dozen of their best canvases in the picture gallery. That will settle the argument. But meanwhile, we have work to do.

She approaches the HEAD WAITER.

DUCHESS. Ferdinand, we need your help. That is why I asked you to come here. The Prince has not yet had the opportunity of being presented to this young lady, and I am determined that when he sees her, he shall be thunderstruck. Absolutely thunderstruck! But, alas, we cannot work miracles. It would be so much easier if we could—frankly, we need one.
AMANDA. Oh, don't say that, madame! I'm scared enough as it is!
DUCHESS. There's no sense in minimizing the difficulties of our task, dear. We have a physical resemblance. That goes a long way, but not far enough, especially in the case of a woman like Léocadia. We must create an atmosphere. First of all—(*to* HECTOR)—where are the orchids?
HECTOR (*jumping up, as though afraid that he might have been sitting on them*). The orchids!
DUCHESS. Have you forgotten that Léocadia never went anywhere without a sheaf of orchids? I must telephone Dinard and have a selection sent along immediately.

She goes out. He follows. AMANDA *is left alone with the* HEAD WAITER. *They look at each other for a moment, embarrassed. Then she says, with a smile:*

AMANDA. Phantasmagoric, am I . . .?

He hesitates, as though unsure what attitude to take—then makes a vague and non-committal gesture.

We've got a funny profession, you and I, haven't we?

HEAD WAITER (*stiff and formal*). There is no such thing as a funny profession, mademoiselle.

AMANDA (*gently*). No, I suppose there isn't. (*Pause.*) Well, we all have to eat, don't we? How long have you been at it?

HEAD WAITER. At what, mademoiselle?

AMANDA. Being a memory.

HEAD WAITER. Nearly two years now, mademoiselle.

AMANDA. D'you get decent pay?

The HEAD WAITER *is shocked by this question. He makes a gesture reminiscent of a butler refusing a tip.*

HEAD WAITER. Mademoiselle!

Then, abashed by AMANDA'S *clear gaze, he adds:*

Yes, mademoiselle, very good pay. . . .

At once he is overcome with remorse at having given away forbidden secrets of his profession. He adds shamefacedly:

Well . . . that is . . . when I say 'good' . . . I don't mean. . . .

AMANDA (*amused at his embarrassment*). Is it tiring?

HEAD WAITER. What, mademoiselle?

AMANDA. Being a memory.

The HEAD WAITER *makes a negative gesture.*

What do you do all day?

HEAD WAITER. Nothing. I just wait. I wait for him to come. I walk about among the empty tables. I think.

He adds, in a burst of confidence:

It's strange, isn't it, when you consider it. Strange, and a bit sad, really.

AMANDA. I only saw him for a moment last night—and it was very dark. What's he like? Is he nice?

HEAD WAITER. He's neither nice nor not nice. He just doesn't seem to be there at all, if you know what I mean.

AMANDA. What does he do when he comes into your restaurant?

HEAD WAITER. He sits down at a table—always the same one—the table they had that night. Then he orders what they ordered then—a bottle of Pommery '47. I bring the champagne and two glasses. Then he sits and stares at the empty chair opposite him, without saying a word. Sometimes all night. And then he goes away.

AMANDA (*dreamy*). Poor chap.

HEAD WAITER. And we drink the champagne.

AMANDA (*ingenuous*). Ooh! Aren't you lucky!

HEAD WAITER. I don't know so much about that, mademoiselle. It's beginning to affect my liver....

AMANDA (*after a pause*). What's so funny is that they only knew each other for three days. I should have thought it took longer than that to fall in love ... properly, I mean....

Suddenly she demands of the HEAD WAITER:

Were they lovers?

HEAD WAITER (*after his first shocked reaction*). That I can't say, mademoiselle. They certainly didn't spend the night together in *my* establishment.

Pause. Unbending a little ...

The people who run the Chime of Bells—they've been brought here too, you know—they maintain ... but then I have reason to believe that they circulate the story simply to try to look important themselves....

AMANDA (*very soft*). And even if they were lovers ... they had so little time together ... just one night.... (*Urgent again.*) Do you think he's *really* heartbroken, really and truly?

The HEAD WAITER *indicates by a gesture that he does not intend to commit himself.*

I know people do suffer terribly from broken hearts. But I always thought that they either bottled it all up so that nobody knew about it, or else went really crazy. I've never known anyone behave as he does.

HEAD WAITER (*infinitely lofty and patronizing*). How can one presume to analyse the grief of the aristocracy, mademoiselle? I remember before the war at Monte Carlo seeing the Grand Duke Sosthène, in an excess of neurasthenia, empty three hundred magnums of Veuve Cliquot, chateau-bottled, on to the floor of his private sitting-room in the hotel, and force all the members of the staff to wash their feet in it. Then he burst into tears, beat his breast, and begged our pardon most profusely.

AMANDA (*soft*). I don't believe that was real grief. . . .

The DUCHESS *has returned, followed by* HECTOR.

DUCHESS. There! Two hundred orchids will be here in ten minutes.

AMANDA (*smiling*). Surely that's far too many?

DUCHESS (*turning surprised*). What do you mean, too many?

AMANDA. I may not know much about painters, madame, but I do know about flowers. I used to work for a florist before I went into millinery.

DUCHESS. Too many? I very much doubt whether it will be enough. Léocadia used to nibble them ceaselessly. How long do you think it takes a person of sensitivity to nibble the heart out of an orchid—naturally, she discarded the outside petals?

AMANDA. I've no idea. If I wanted to eat flowers, I'd buy daisies. They're cheaper.

DUCHESS (*not even hearing this last remark*). Now, we must plan. I have decided to reconstruct a specific incident for the child. I think that the arrival of Léocadia at the Blue Danube restaurant would be the most vivid.

She seizes a chair.

First of all, we must set the scene. (*To* AMANDA.) Sit there for a moment. (*To* HECTOR.) Isn't she ravishing? And she is getting the idea of it already.

She inspects AMANDA'S *face at very close quarters, and adds:*

Ravishing!

AMANDA. I suppose I'd better try to look distinguished.

DUCHESS (*bustling away*). No, no. Don't try to look anything. We will tell you what to do. (*To the* HEAD WAITER.) I don't want to rehearse in your café, because Albert is in the park and he might come in and catch us at it. Here we are perfectly safe. He never comes into the house in the morning, and in any case Theophilus is keeping watch at the door. Right.

She goes to AMANDA.

DUCHESS. Now, child, I have come to the conclusion that the secret of Léocadia's fascination lay in her eyes. She had a way of looking at one—something like this—which was absolutely irresistible. Between ourselves, she was extremely short-sighted. While we are arranging the furniture, I want you to practise screwing up your eyes, as I showed you. . . . (*To the* HEAD WAITER.) You can help me move this negro. Léocadia loved him. She always called him her coal-black Ariel, as fickle and insubstantial as a fugitive shadow. . . .

She lifts the figure with the aid of the HEAD WAITER.

Heavens, what a heavy brute he is.

As she passes AMANDA, *she says:*

Screw up your eyes, child. Screw up your eyes and incline your head slightly forward. That's better. You're coming on splendidly.

The door half-opens noiselessly, the BUTLER *peeps in, and is shattered to see that his rival, aided by the* DUCHESS, *is flaunting the most sacred conventions of the drawing room by moving the statue, while in a corner the strange young person is screwing up her eyes and bowing her head incessantly, and for no apparent reason. He trembles with horror and disappears.*

DUCHESS (*rearranging the furniture*). If this is the stage where the orchestra is, then the table where they sat should go here. Is that right?

HEAD WAITER. Approximately, yes, Your Grace.

DUCHESS. Well done. (*As the* HEAD WAITER *looks up in surprise.*) I was talking to myself. (*To* AMANDA.) Stop screwing up your eyes now, child, you'll get cramp, and the knack will desert you when you need it most. (*To the* HEAD WAITER.) Now I will tell you what I want you to do. I knew Léocadia too well. It would be of the greatest value to us if you, as a stranger, would describe to the young lady your instinctive, overwhelming impression of the divine Léocadia when she entered the Blue Danube nightclub for the first time.

HEAD WAITER (*delighted to be asked to play such an important rôle*). My impression?

DUCHESS. Your instinctive impression. Don't be afraid. Take your time. We are all comrades here, seeking only to unearth the truth, the whole truth and nothing but the truth.

HEAD WAITER (*instinctively raising his hand*). So help me God.

DUCHESS. What's that?

HEAD WAITER (*blushing*). Nothing, Your Grace. Forgive me.

DUCHESS. Very well. We are waiting. (*To* AMANDA.) I said stop screwing up your eyes, girl. For heaven's sake, stop!

AMANDA (*whose eyes are screwed up in a desperate effort to hide her laughter*). I didn't know I was doing it, madame.

DUCHESS (*delighted*). Excellent! You are really beginning to feel like Léocadia. In that case, screw them up by all means, dear. (*To the* HEAD WAITER.) We are still waiting.

HEAD WAITER (*who has had time to think it over*). Very well then. To be honest, Your Grace, when Mademoiselle Léocadia Gardi first came into the Blue Danube, I think I am speaking for all of us there when I say that we received a profound shock.

DUCHESS. A shock? How very interesting. A shock. (*To* AMANDA.) Remember that, child. Have you a pencil?

AMANDA (*who can hardly suppress her mirth*). No, but I'll remember. (*Imitating the* HEAD WAITER.) A shock.

DUCHESS (*repeats, entranced*). A shock.

HEAD WAITER. A shock. First of all, Mademoiselle Léocadia was beautiful—very beautiful indeed. And then, she had a most disturbing way of looking you straight in the eyes, walking right up to you, and then looking away at the very moment when you expected her to speak to you . . . she did it with an air of arrogance, of distinction . . . which reminded me more than anything of . . . may I speak frankly, Your Grace?

DUCHESS. Please do.

HEAD WAITER. A dog! A mad dog! A demented Borzoi!

DUCHESS (*enthusiastic*). A demented Borzoi! (*To* AMANDA.) Remember all that. It is surprisingly accurate. This fellow has a rare and courageous gift of observation. It's quite true—the whole of Léocadia's character was revealed in that particular and inimitable manner of walking.

She demonstrates.

Holding your eyes with hers until your noses were in imminent danger of collison, and then—suddenly—losing interest and passing you by without another glance. There is her whole personality in a nutshell. I am quite different of course. With my height, I have to stand on tiptoe to look anybody in the eyes. (*To the* HEAD WAITER.) Do you know what you must do now, my good man, to make a lasting impression on the child? You must give us a demonstration.

HEAD WAITER. A demonstration of what, Your Grace?

DUCHESS. Of Léocadia entering the Blue Danube, of course.

HEAD WAITER (*who is dying to*). I really don't know if I can, Your Grace. . . .

DUCHESS. It is an order.

HEAD WAITER. Very good, Your Grace. But Your Grace must understand that I mean no disrespect by anything I do . . . after all, I'm a man . . . it's not easy for a man to imitate a lady. . . .

DUCHESS. Don't worry about that. We are here simply and solely to build up an atmosphere for the girl.

HEAD WAITER. All right, then. When Mademoiselle Léocadia Gardi came in, the orchestra had just started to play, by special request, a number which was very popular that year—'The First Bouquet'.

DUCHESS. One moment! I have an idea. Hector, you can be the orchestra. Go up on the stage—that's right. You know 'The First Bouquet'—two years ago you nearly drove us all mad whistling it. Hum it. It will help this good fellow.

HECTOR (*delighted*). May I mime the violinist as well?
DUCHESS) *uninterested*). If you wish.

> HECTOR *hums a catchy waltz to himself and debates mimically upon the desirability or otherwise of accompanying himself upon an imaginary violin.*

HEAD WAITER. If you are agreeable, Your Grace, I will direct my entrance at you.
DUCHESS. An excellent idea.
HEAD WAITER. Right! Orchestra!

> HECTOR *attacks 'The First Bouquet'. The* HEAD WAITER, *with great seriousness, begins to mime Léocadia's entry into the Blue Danube. At this moment, the* BUTLER *enters precipitately, much agitated.*

BUTLER. Your Grace!

> *He stops, rooted to the spot, as his rival passes him, oblivious and apparently performing the steps of some outlandish tango, with his eyes fixed hypnotically on those of the* DUCHESS, *who exclaims as he reaches her:*

DUCHESS. That's it! That's it! That's absolutely right! This man is a mimic—a born mimic! Do it again, quickly, while you are in the mood. And you, child, walk behind him and copy everything he does.

> HECTOR *starts the waltz again. The* HEAD WAITER *repeats his performance, with* AMANDA, *who is bursting with laughter, following behind and imitating him. The* HEAD WAITER *finishes his promenade and turns to watch his pupil. He cries ecstatically:*

HEAD WAITER. Bravo, mademoiselle! Just like that! Now, come right up to me—look me in the eye! Be arrogant! Be haughty! I'm only a Head Waiter! I'm lower than mud! You don't even see me any more!

But AMANDA *has suddenly stopped dead, covered in confusion. For the* PRINCE *has pushed aside the* BUTLER, *who since his entrance has stood as though petrified, and stands there in the doorway, pale with anger.* HECTOR *stops humming, and the* DUCHESS *and the* HEAD WAITER *turn round, dumbfounded.*

PRINCE. Aunt Melisande!
DUCHESS. Albert!
PRINCE. What is the meaning of this masquerade?
DUCHESS. Theophilus, what have you done?
BUTLER (*looking ten years older, as he bows his head*). I came to warn Your Grace, but I was so dumbfounded by what I saw that I fear I——
DUCHESS (*terrible, with an imperious gesture*). Theophilus, you are dismissed!

The BUTLER *creeps out, a hundred years older.*

PRINCE (*dry, to the others*). Perhaps the rest of you would be kind enough to leave us also. I must speak to this young lady alone.

HECTOR and the HEAD WAITER *beat a hasty retreat. The* DUCHESS *also prepares to go. The* PRINCE *looks at* AMANDA *for the first time, to her great embarrassment. Suddenly he sees the Venetian negro. He leaps to it.*

Who has dared to lay hands on this statue?
DUCHESS (*at the door*). I did, Albert. I wished to clear a space for——
PRINCE (*in a fury, as he puts the statue back in its original place*). I gave orders that nobody, under any pretext whatsoever, was to touch anything that she had touched!

The DUCHESS, *who is really not very intimidated by this display of temper, is making complicated signs to*

>AMANDA *behind the* PRINCE'S *back. He studies* AMANDA *silently. The* DUCHESS *goes.*

PRINCE. I am afraid that my aunt has placed you in an embarrassing position, mademoiselle.

AMANDA (*simple*). I'm afraid she has, sir.

PRINCE (*unkind*). I don't doubt that you were desperate to find employment of some sort——

AMANDA. No, sir. That is to say, yes, sir. You see, your aunt had taken the trouble to get me dismissed from the milliner's where I worked before she summoned me here.

PRINCE (*amused*). She's an amazing woman.

AMANDA (*a little bitter*). Amazing is right. (*Pause.*) But since yesterday I've got to the point where nothing amazes me any more.

PRINCE. You have been here since yesterday?

AMANDA. Yes. You even spoke to me last night, in the park, by that obelisk with the stone bench round it——

PRINCE. Was that you? I must beg your pardon for not recognizing you. It was very dark. Why did you ask me the way to the sea?

AMANDA (*soft*). Apparently that was the particular phrase of which you had to be . . . reminded. . . .

>*The* PRINCE *stops as though thunderstruck, and murmurs:*

PRINCE. Excuse me, can you tell me the way to the sea?

>*He sits down in an arm-chair, saying nothing, as if in a trance. Endless pause.* AMANDA *clears her throat. No effect. She starts to tiptoe out. He suddenly cries:*

PRINCE. Don't go! Come back, where I can see you! You are plain. You walk badly. You are not in the least like her. You never could be like her. You're just a common little milliner, with no mystery, no aura——

AMANDA. What's that?

PRINCE (*stops surprised*). What?

AMANDA. An aura?

PRINCE (*exploding*). If you imagine that I'm going to give you lessons in your own language into the bargain——!

AMANDA (*looking him straight in the face. With dignity*). I only wanted to know if it's an insult.

PRINCE (*looking at her, he cannot repress a little smile. He says quietly*). No, it is not an insult.

AMANDA. I'm glad.

> Pause. She looks him up and down and then walks towards the door with as much dignity as she can muster. The PRINCE cannot help asking:

PRINCE. What would you have done if it had been an insult?

AMANDA (*turning*). I would have told you just what I think of you.

PRINCE (*quiet and suddenly very weary*). I don't care what anybody thinks of me.

> He retires into his huge old-fashioned arm-chair and relapses into silence.
> AMANDA *watches him from the doorway with a suspicion of pity in her eyes. Suddenly he begins to mutter with closed eyes:*

PRINCE. Can you tell me——?

> He stops, then tries again in a different tone.

Can you tell me the way——?

> He tries another tone, but his voice is not flexible.

... the way to ...

> He stops, weary. His features relax in sheer exhaustion. Tears come into AMANDA'S eyes as she sees that he is

really distraught, and she murmurs softly, as she did in the park:

AMANDA. Can you tell me the way to the sea?

Pause.

PRINCE (*soft, almost humble*). Who taught you to imitate that voice?

AMANDA. Nobody. It's my own voice.

PRINCE (*after a pause*). Would you mind very much repeating that sentence once more?

AMANDA. Excuse me, can you tell me the way to the sea?

PRINCE (*soft, eyes closed*). The second turning on the left, mademoiselle.

AMANDA. Thank you.

PRINCE (*eyes still closed—suddenly*). Mademoiselle——

AMANDA (*surprised*). Yes?

PRINCE. You have dropped your glove.

AMANDA looks at her feet, surprised, and then realizes that he is reliving his conversation of two years ago. Timidly, hazarding a guess, she says:

AMANDA. Thank you. That is very kind of you.

PRINCE (*opening his eyes*). No. She didn't answer me. She just smiled, a tantalizing half-smile, and disappeared into the dusk.

He stands up, not looking at her. Suddenly he puts a hand to his eye, as though to wipe away a tear.

Forgive me.

AMANDA. It's you who must forgive me for being here.

Pause. AMANDA *looks at him, then says gravely:*

What I don't understand is that last night I said the very same thing to you in the same tone of voice, and you answered me quite calmly, as though I—oh, I don't know —as though it was the most ordinary thing in the world for someone to stand there in the twilight and ask you the way to the sea.

PRINCE. That's strange, isn't it?

AMANDA. Yes. It is strange.

PRINCE (*with difficulty, not looking at her*). Mademoiselle, I wonder whether—in spite of what I have said to you—in spite of what you must think of me—you would consider accepting my aunt's proposition, and for a little while— say for three days—you would . . .

> AMANDA *bows her head. With all the dignity she can manage, she says:*

AMANDA. Last night, I refused. This morning, I said 'yes'. Just now I was on the point of going out to say 'no' again. . . .

PRINCE (*turning to her, kindly, for the first time*). Please say 'yes' again. It will make the score even.

AMANDA. But it makes me look such a fool, always changing my mind.

PRINCE. And how will I look?

AMANDA. Oh, but—it doesn't matter for you. I can't afford the luxury of going nuts about anybody at the moment.

PRINCE. And what would happen to you if you did 'go nuts', as you say, about someone?

AMANDA. Oh, dreadful things! I'd ladder my stockings and lose my gloves and miss my train and lose my job——

She stops and sighs, laughing in spite of herself.

Anyway, all those things did happen to me yesterday.

PRINCE (*on the defensive*). You have doubtless heard my story. I agree that for someone who leads your sort of existence, in which your job and the small material considerations of everyday life loom so importantly, it must be somewhat galling to think of so much money, time and trouble expended on the worship of a memory.

AMANDA (*quiet and simple*). Oh, no, you're quite wrong. When we got the telegram saying that my father would never come back from the war, my mother, who was just an ordinary housewife, went and slept on a camp-bed in the kitchen. And in the room that they had shared, she laid out everything that had belonged to him—she put his best suit, the one he was married in—on the bed next to her white wedding dress, and every year, on the anniversary of his death, the flowers she used to buy cost her far more—comparatively—than you could ever spend even if you rebuilt a whole town in your park.

PRINCE. I beg your pardon.

AMANDA (*very kind*). Granted. But I don't want you to think——

PRINCE. I no longer think it, mademoiselle. And I am profoundly grateful to you for what you have just told me, because it makes it possible for me to confide in you—a terrible confidance which I have never before entrusted to anyone. My aunt is a lunatic—a charming lunatic perhaps—but a lunatic all the same. I am saner than she is, I assure you. The only reason I have submitted to the caprices of her folly, and allowed her to rebuild in the privacy of the estate every house that I visited with Léocadia—the only reason was the hope that this very privacy and isolation would help me a little in my terrible struggle.

AMANDA (*bewildered*). Your struggle?

PRINCE (*with a smile*). Yes. It's extraordinarily difficult to tell you this. And now that I am on the point of making my confession, I can see that it is almost comic. But please don't laugh at me . . . I agreed to all this simply because I am on the verge of forgetting.

AMANDA. Forgetting what?

PRINCE. The woman I loved. I can't even remember the

exact colour of her eyes. I had completely forgotten her voice until just now ... last night I was in the clouds. ...

He taps his forehead.

To think that you could have stood there, in the same twilight, and asked me in that very voice the way to the sea ... and I didn't cry out ... I wasn't even surprised. ... I simply didn't notice. It's terrible. ... it's laughable ... Prince Albert Troubiscoi rebuilds a whole town in his park to preserve the memory of his love, and then he can't even remember the first words she said to him. ...

He sits down, worn out.

AMANDA. How can I help you, sir?

PRINCE (*low after a pause*). Stay here for three days, and let me watch you moving through those memory-ridden haunts where I seek for her, in vain. Try—forgive me for saying this—but please try to be not yourself, but her—just for three days.

AMANDA (*who is standing with one hand caressing the Venetian negro*). I will try.

PRINCE (*a sudden cry*). Stay there! Don't move, I beg you. ... (*Reminiscent.*) The next day she came to this house after luncheon to ask my aunt if she would lend the park for a charity fête. My aunt was out, and so the butler called me. ... I found her in here ... standing just like that ... she told me she loved that statue ... we spent the whole afternoon together, and that evening she allowed me to take her to the Blue Danube for the first time. That was the restaurant where, the following evening, we discovered that we loved each other. ...

His eyes are closed.

PRINCE. The Blue Danube. The most pretentious and ridiculous place in the world. With that fantastic head waiter, and that ghastly mock-Viennese music, which everyone was raving about that year . . . she hummed it to herself all the evening. . . .

He makes a poor attempt to sing the opening bars of the waltz.

Tra-la-la . . . how does that waltz go?

He tries again.

Tra-la-la. . . .
AMANDA (*helping him*). Tra-la-la. . . .
PRINCE (*bolder*). Tra-la-la . . . *la!*

AMANDA finishes the phrase. Then they repeat the chorus together. The orchestra takes up the melody, which swells up into a joyous burst of music as the lights dim, and then come up again upon . . .

ACT THREE

The clearing in the park where the DUCHESS *has rebuilt the Blue Danube café, which is brilliantly lit, the sparkling radiance from its tinkling chandeliers illuminating the old-fashioned charm of its baroque red plush and gilt décor. Three* GIPSIES, *who vaguely resemble skating instructors, ply their violins assiduously. They remind one of ancient, dusty moths—once brilliant creatures of the night, now mouldering neglected in a glass case, transfixed by pins. Indeed, so do the* HEAD WAITER *and the* CLOAKROOM ATTENDANT—*the latter with her bun and frilly apron looking like a superannuated usherette.* AMANDA *and the* PRINCE *have just arrived, and the* CLOAKROOM ATTENDANT, *ravished with delight, is helping* AMANDA *off with her furs. The* HEAD WAITER *hovers expectantly. They sit down at their table.*

HEAD WAITER (*as if he didn't know*). And what may I bring you, sir?

PRINCE. The same as last night.

HEAD WAITER. Very good, sir.

He writes down on his pad.

Pommery, '47.

AMANDA (*without thinking*). Oh . . . first of all . . . I would awfully like . . . I mean, I'm terribly thirsty, I do love it . . . a gin and lime with lots of water.

There is a moment of utter dismay. The music stops.

HEAD WAITER. But . . . that is . . . Mademoiselle Gardi did not . . . I'm sorry, mademoiselle, but. . . .

AMANDA (*in confusion*). No, no, *I'm* sorry. I must be crazy. Champagne . . . of course. The same as last night. Champagne it is.

The music starts again, relieved.

PRINCE (*stiff, after a pause*). If you are really thirsty . . . and if you're so very fond of it . . . bring a gin and lime for mademoiselle.

HEAD WAITER (*stunned*). A gin and lime. I'll go and see if we . . . yes, very good, sir. . . .

AMANDA (*calling after him*). With lots of water, please!

HEAD WAITER (*more and more shocked*). Water! I've never heard of such a thing. . . . I suppose we can melt some ice. . . .

AMANDA. Thank you—you're very kind. I'll drink it up quickly.

HEAD WAITER (*as he goes, sotto voce*). I should hope so, and when I've removed the glass we will never refer to the incident again.

AMANDA (*with an apologetic smile*). It's very difficult, you know, to have no will of one's own for two whole days.

PRINCE (*dry*). Please try to be patient. The day after to-morrow you will be free.

AMANDA. I don't need to be patient, you know that. It's thrilling being somebody else. . . .

She fingers her bracelets.

Somebody rich . . . somebody in love. . . .

Meanwhile, the gin and lime is being prepared—an elaborate and complicated ritual involving large numbers of people and much coming and going. The CLOAKROOM ATTENDANT *and one of the* GIPSIES *who has temporarily abandoned his violin join in the proceedings, which develop into a kind of furtive ballet, underlined by an impertinent musical score which twists the still-recognizable theme of the waltz into an ironic commentary. At last, the precious glass is ready, and the* HEAD WAITER *brings it to the table.*

PRINCE. You weren't at all bad yesterday.

HEAD WAITER. Your gin and lime, mademoiselle.

He adds, with malice, for this is what upset him most:

With lots of water.

AMANDA (*who really is thirsty*). Oh, thank you!

She takes a mouthful and then suddenly looks at the glass.

Ooh, it's lovely and strong!

She seems to be on the point of enjoying herself genuinely, revelling in the unaccustomed lights, music, perfume and jewels. But suddenly she notices that the PRINCE *and the* HEAD WAITER *are watching her with icy impatience. Hastily she empties the glass in a single gulp, and cannot hide a grimace at the unwonted strength of the drink.*

AMANDA. Pardon.

She gives the glass to the HEAD WAITER, *who takes it with a satisfied sigh.*

HEAD WAITER. Ah!

PRINCE (*also relieved that this interlude is over*). Ah!

The orchestra, which had suspended operations during the sacriligious moment, breaks out again into the most sentimental version of the waltz theme, and the HEAD WAITER *brings on the champagne bucket and serves it with all the ceremony fitting to a serious occasion, in an atmosphere restored to serenity.*

PRINCE. Yesterday was not at all bad, for a first attempt, in spite of a few mistakes, and—how can I put it without wounding you?—a trace of the... plebeian in your manner, which, I must admit, is not without a certain charm of its own, but which, naturally, strikes the wrong note.

AMANDA. I haven't said a single word of slang all day.

PRINCE (*off-hand, to* AMANDA'S *horror*). That's true. Of course, Léocadia spoke nothing but slang—but it would be asking too much to expect you to reproduce her language as well ... and in any case, we said very little to each other, that first evening. The important thing was to see you sitting there, on the other side of the table, nibbling your flowers.

AMANDA (*apologetically*). I'm afraid I'm not much good with the flowers. I'm getting a bit discouraged about it.

PRINCE. Discouraged?

AMANDA. Yes. Oh, I love to suck juicy blades of grass out in the fields, but these great big flowers ... they're bitter and sweet all at the same time ... and having bits of them in my mouth all the evening—it's ... well ...

PRINCE (*dreamy*). She used to say that they reminded her of opium-poppy and mandragora, and all the baleful draughts of the inscrutable Orient.

AMANDA (*trying to raise a smile from the* HEAD WAITER, *who is watching her icily*). I don't know anything about those things. I only know orchids give me a stomach ache. But I was better this afternoon, wasn't I?

PRINCE. Much better. Perhaps you feel that I was not over-lavish with my compliments to you, mademoiselle?

AMANDA. You certainly weren't.

PRINCE. Well, I can tell you now that this afternoon, when we took the boat and idled away the long sunlit hours exploring the upper reaches of the river, your evocation of the divine spirit of Léocadia was very nearly faultless.

AMANDA (*pleased, with a triumphant look at the* HEAD WAITER). Thank you.

PRINCE (*without malice*). Of course, I realize that on that afternoon two years ago she deliberately dimmed the radiance of her blazing intellect to harmonize with my mood.

AMANDA (*deflated*). Thank you all the same.

She avoids the eye of the HEAD WAITER, *who goes out with a mocking grin.*

PRINCE (*oblivious*). Yes, you were quite perfect. A touch livelier than she perhaps . . . a little too much flesh-and-blood.

AMANDA. It's very difficult to be anything else when one *is* alive. But I'll do better this evening! I feel so light, as if I'm hardly weighing on my chair at all . . . but that's no wonder, considering the meals we've been having.

PRINCE. Léocadia always laid her glove down on her plate.

AMANDA. I know . . . lucky I've got plenty of pairs of gloves. . . . (*Afterthought.*) One day, you know, I'll eat one of them.

PRINCE (*regarding her dreamily*). Léocadia, blessed spirit . . . (*To* AMANDA.) I beg of you, mademoiselle, out of respect to her sacred spectre . . . even if your natural appetite overcomes you—as it must, as it has every right to—even if you do order huge meals to be sent up to your room each night after we have parted, I pray you, do not tell me about them.

AMANDA (*her eyes downcast*). I may be only flesh and blood, but I am honest. I really am trying, however hard it may be, to be like her for these three days—even when I'm not with you. I promise you I've eaten nothing but orchids and champagne, and my plate has been absolutely empty except for embroidered gloves! I generally go to bed at eight, but last night I sat up as late as Mademoiselle Gardi used to. If you'd walked past my window, you'd have seen me there in the small hours lying on a gilt chaise-longue like she did, and trying—unsuccessfully, I'm afraid—to read the poems of Mallarmé by candlelight. It was terribly uncomfortable.

PRINCE (*very surprised*). But why? You knew there was not the remotest chance that I would pass your window after I had formally bidden you 'goodnight'. Did you do it for fun?

AMANDA. I should say not! I like books that make me laugh, and I like to sleep. . . . Oh, how I'm going to sleep the day after tomorrow!

PRINCE. Then—why?

AMANDA (*a little ill at ease*). Because . . . well, when I do a job, I like to do it properly, that's all.

Pause. They have moved closer together, unconsciously. The GIPSIES *feel obliged to strike up a gay Viennese number. When the* PRINCE *begins to speak again, they finish the music softly, and sit down again.*

PRINCE (*reverting to his original idea*). That second evening was the turning-point of our lives . . . that is, of all the life which was left to us. A precious morning together, and a last valedictory afternoon. . . .

AMANDA. That was the evening when you discovered you loved each other, wasn't it?

PRINCE (*brusque*). Who told you that?

AMANDA. I can't remember—you, I think.

PRINCE. No, not me.

AMANDA. Then it must have been your aunt—or perhaps I just sensed it when we arrived here tonight.

PRINCE. Yes, it was on the second evening. And as that strange night wore on—superficially like so many other nights, with soft lights and music, with wine and conversation, we——

AMANDA (*interrupting*). What did you talk about that night, before you began talking about yourselves?

PRINCE. We talked of nothing but ourselves . . . we may have mentioned the subtle colours of the river at sunset, our favourite poets, her hats, the people around us who made us laugh . . . but we were talking about ourselves all the time. . . .

AMANDA. Did you do the talking, or did she?

PRINCE. Well . . . both of us . . . perhaps she more than I . . . why did you ask me that?

AMANDA (*shrinking into her red plush chair, says shyly, after a pause*). No reason . . . just that it seemed to me. . . if I had fallen in love with you after that long sunny afternoon on the river, I'd have wanted to sit quite still, feeling the smooth satin of my dress against my sunburnt skin, and the cool touch of diamonds on my arm, and the icy stem of my glass between my fingers . . . and just looked at you without saying a word.

PRINCE (*calmly*). That is because you are a young savage, incapable of analysing your own emotions.

AMANDA. I suppose I am.

PRINCE. Of course you are. And your attempts at self-analysis would undoubtedly have been hopelessly inept. Which reminds me, I meant to thank you for the perfect tact and discretion with which you have played your part up till now. I presume that you are not talkative by nature?

AMANDA. Oh, but I am. The other girls in the workshop called me 'Chinwag'.

PRINCE (*adjusting his monocle*). Chinwag?

AMANDA. Yes, because I never stopped talking.

PRINCE. In that case, you must have great natural tact, which is even better.

AMANDA (*laughing*). Oh, goodness, no! In the shop where I was before, they used to call me Flatfoot.

PRINCE. Flatfoot?

AMANDA. Because I was always putting my foot in things.

PRINCE. You do not appear to me to deserve either of those nicknames.

AMANDA (*laughs*). Oh, I do . . . that's why I'd be so pleased if I made a success of these three days. And if I can't talk like Mademoiselle Léocadia, I do at least want to keep silent in the same way that she did. There are so many different ways of saying nothing to the man you love. How did she say nothing to you?

PRINCE. She spoke a little less loudly.

AMANDA (*stupefied*). But she went on speaking?

PRINCE. Oh, yes. She would always answer her own questions, or else finish your reply for you. At other times, she just murmured words at random—in Rumanian, as a rule—that was her mother-tongue. That uninterrupted monologue, revealing every facet of her agile personality, those continual conversational fireworks, were one of her greatest charms. She would punctuate her talk with deep, fascinating ripples of throaty laughter, thrown into the conversation at the moment when they were least expected, and dying away into what was almost a sob.

AMANDA. I must seem very dull beside her.

PRINCE. No, no. Naturally nobody could expect you to emulate her verbal genius. You have done very well, mademoiselle, to present me with such an accurate and precious picture of her rare moments of silence.

He has taken her hand quite naturally towards the end of this speech. Now he suddenly drops it.

I beg your pardon.

AMANDA (*looking at her hand*). For what?

PRINCE. I took your hand. She hated anybody to touch her.

AMANDA. Even you?

PRINCE. Especially me. She used to say that I had coarse peasant hands—hands made to hurt and destroy.

AMANDA (*taking his hand quickly and looking at it*). Peasant hands?

PRINCE (*a little embarrassed*). The skin is hard, I know. But what with yachting and tennis . . . and then, I don't know if you agree with me, but I simply cannot play golf in gloves. . . .

AMANDA (*still looking at his hand*). How funny. You're a gentleman of leisure, and yet your hand does look like a peasant's. Hold out your arm so I can see it properly.

He holds out his arm, a little surprised. She shuts her eyes and after a pause, murmurs:

No. They are hard, but they would never do anybody any harm.

The PRINCE *takes away his hand. Pause. The* GIPSIES, *terrified of being caught red-handed in idleness, leap to their violins. The Leader comes to the table, playing his seductive melody. The* PRINCE *says nothing, but stares at his hand. After a moment,* AMANDA *ventures timidly:*

AMANDA. Penny for your thoughts?

PRINCE. I was thinking . . . if she had said—that evening— what you have just said—about my hands—I would have been wild with happiness.

AMANDA (*soft*). But if she talked so much, she must have told you, among other things, that she loved you.

PRINCE (*suddenly hanging his head like an embarrassed boy*).

Oh, yes. But she was so adept at self-analysis, at pinning down the most fleeting and fugitive nuance of her vagabond spirit under the microscope of her intelligence, that I find it extremely difficult to remember the exact words she used to declare her love——

AMANDA. Not the exact words, perhaps—but you surely remember the moment when she said them.

PRINCE. Even that is difficult. She was crazy that evening —she started a thousand topics—tossed them into the air and caught them as they fell in cascades of coloured stars. She played at being every great lover in mythology—she compared me to a bull—to a swan. She even made me light an enormous cigar—a thing I detest—because she swore that some goddess or other was raped by Jupiter disguised as a puff of smoke! And all this intermingled with reminiscences of the ballets she had danced. That night I was Daphnis and Prince Siegfried, Jupiter and Mars. . . .

The violinist has rejoined his fellows, and the music dies softly into silence. AMANDA *asks in a small voice:*

AMANDA. But you are sure that she didn't once say, simply, 'I love you'?

PRINCE (*amused*). Léocadia was incapable of saying simply 'I love you'—even to her favourite greyhound or the little tame serpent which followed her everywhere.

AMANDA. I'm not talking about a little serpent, tame or not! I'm talking about you! I can't bear to think that she never said 'I love you, Albert'.

PRINCE (*sarcastic*). 'I love you, Albert'! Really, mademoiselle, you are ludicrous. Please get it into your head once and for all that this was not a flirtation between a shop girl and a butcher's boy on a park bench.

AMANDA. That's quite obvious. (*Trying to console him,*

gently.) I expect she did say 'I love you' among all the other things, and you just didn't hear it.

PRINCE. I don't think so.

AMANDA. But when you come here in the evenings, and try to imagine her sitting here opposite you, don't you imagine her talking?

PRINCE (*heavy*). Of course ... not straight away ... it takes me several hours before I can conjure up the picture of her sitting there motionless ... she used to move about such a lot! And even then, there are details which evade me ... the eyes.... I can never quite remember the eyes....

AMANDA (*soft*). You can see them tonight.

PRINCE. When I have built up a complete picture of her in my mind, then, very cautiously, I imagine her talking...

AMANDA (*unable to refrain from a slightly malicious note*). You imagine the monologue, do you?

PRINCE (*ingenuous*). Oh, no, that would be far too difficult —almost impossible. And then—the sweet ghost I conjure up is so fragile—like thistledown—a puff of wind, a tiny incongruous sound—and she vanishes.... I have to imagine her saying the simplest things ... 'Yes ... no ... perhaps ... this evening'. I try to make her say my name ... she decorated me with a galaxy of ridiculous nicknames, you see ... Florizel, Endymion, Prince Charming ... she never called me by my real name—she found it unaesthetic ... which it is, of course—but still, it is my name. So now I take my gentle revenge—I make her say 'Albert'. Once I sat here for a whole night, making her repeat over and over again 'My darling Albert'. But I am hoist with my own petard, for the only time she ever said that to me, she was making fun of me, and it is always that moment which I recapture when I visualize her lips forming my name.

AMANDA. And do you never make her say 'I love you'?

That would be the moment when you had her in your power.

PRINCE (*lowering his eyes, embarrassed*). No. I dare not. And I cannot really imagine that she ever did say it ... I have no recollection of her lips forming those words.

AMANDA (*almost tenderly*). Look at me.

He raises his head, surprised, and looks at her. Looking him straight in the eyes, she murmurs softly:

I love you, Albert.

He looks at her, pale, his face working.

I love you, Albert. Watch my lips, and remember how they look. I love you, Albert.

PRINCE (*a little hard, from a dry throat*). Thank you.

He tries to pour out some champagne but his hand is shaking, and he does not tip the bottle far enough. The HEAD WAITER, *who is hovering like a hawk, misinterprets this, and arrives at the canter.*

HEAD WAITER. Another bottle of champagne, sir?

PRINCE. Yes, please.

The HEAD WAITER *takes the ice-bucket. At once the orchestra, who seem to regard this as a signal, attack a composition of great brio and gaiety. The* PRINCE *turns to them, suddenly angry, and cries:*

No! Stop that music!

The players stop, amazed.

HEAD WAITER (*coming forward*). Forgive me, sir, but surely you have not forgotten that this particular piece of music was played at the exact moment when the second bottle of champagne was served? It was always the custom of this restaurant to start a new number when a fresh bottle of champagne was served. And that is what happened on that particular evening, I can assure you, sir.

PRINCE (*exasperated*). I tell you I don't want to hear that music! I don't care what happened that evening!

There is a shocked silence at these blasphemous words. The HEAD WAITER, *who is holding the ice-pail, trembles like a leaf. In the ghastly pause, the only sound is the rattling of the bottle in the metal bucket. The* PRINCE *and* AMANDA *look at each other, hostile. The* HEAD WAITER *trembles so violently that the champagne, thoroughly shaken up, suddenly expels its cork with a tremendous explosion. The* CLOAKROOM ATTENDANT, *watching from the doorway of her lair, lets out a squeak of alarm. The champagne falls in a deluge of bubbles. The* HEAD WAITER *mops it up, in an agony of mortification.*

HEAD WAITER. Please forgive me, sir. . . . It's the first time in thirty-seven years that that has happened . . . it must have been a bad bottle. I will bring another immediately.

AMANDA (*calmly to the retreating* HEAD WAITER). And another gin and lime for me—with lots of water.

HEAD WAITER (*horrified*). Another gin and lime!

PRINCE (*between clenched teeth, never taking his eyes off her*). What is the meaning of this gratuitous insolence?

AMANDA (*calm*). It's not insolence. It's simply that I don't intend to put up with your stupid bad temper. So I'm going back to being 'me' for a bit. And 'me', I'm thirsty. And 'me', I don't like champagne.

PRINCE. Me! Me! Me! How you love saying that, don't you? Well, let me tell you that for the last two days you've never once stopped being 'you'. You've simply been making fun of something you are too ignorant to understand.

AMANDA. That's not true. I've tried as hard as I can to be her. I've done my level best, and I can't go on a moment longer. Please excuse me, and let me have my gin and lime.
PRINCE. Why did you hurt me by saying those words you knew she never said?
AMANDA. I hoped they would help you.
PRINCE. You're lying.
AMANDA. Yes, I'm lying.

She stands up.

(*Simply.*) Please forgive me what I'm going to say. But it seems to me that a love affair is too precious and beautiful a thing to play about with like this. I know you'll be furious with me, and probably drive me away—but I'll go back to Paris happier if I've told you what I think. She never loved you. But that isn't really important, because you can give all your heart to someone and get nothing in return—and anyway, I'm certain you know already, deep down, that she didn't love you. But there's worse to come, and I must say it before I go. You're young and rich and handsome and charming and your hands aren't really hard... just strong and useful... you ought to try to live, and be happy and forget the past— because I'm absolutely positive that you didn't love her either.

Silence. Nobody breathes. Then the PRINCE *says calmly:*

PRINCE. I'm afraid you are very stupid, mademoiselle, and unspeakably impudent into the bargain. Ferdinand, please bring mademoiselle's wrap. The path back to the house is rather dark, so someone will walk with you. My aunt's secretary will settle up with you in the morning.
AMANDA. You're not hurting anybody but yourself by bringing money into this.

PRINCE (*a bitter smile*). I had quite forgotten the admirably disinterested attitude of the proletariat towards filthy lucre. If you would prefer it, we will pay you nothing.

AMANDA. Oh, yes, you will. You'll give me the price of my return-ticket, and three days' pay as a milliner at trade union rates, with overtime. I can tell you the exact amount.

PRINCE (*icy*). You may go now.

The HEAD WAITER *creeps up, followed by the* CLOAK-ROOM ATTENDANT, *who carries* AMANDA'S *wrap. He stammers with emotion.*

HEAD WAITER. M-M-Mademoiselle's... wr-wrap....

AMANDA. You can take it back to the house yourself. *I* don't wear furs in the summer. *I'm* quite warm enough, thank you.

She moves towards the door with dignity.

PRINCE (*calling her back*). Mademoiselle!

She stops.

Mademoiselle. I belong to a class which is invariably represented in humorous fiction as consisting entirely of effete young half-wits and dithering dotards.... I know I had a strange upbringing at the hands of old ladies and priests. I suppose it's only to be expected that you should think me an imbecile.

AMANDA. I never said that!

PRINCE. But you would have liked to. No, don't deny it, it is quite understandable. I have just accused you of being stupid—we always brand people as imbeciles if their views differ from our own. No. You cannot dispute that people are prejudiced against a man like me, who lives in a sixteenth-century mausoleum, and rejoices in twenty-two Christian names and a procession of titles, all of which lost their significance centuries ago. It may surprise you when I tell you that it is just as difficult for a man in my position to convince people that he is not a blockhead as it would be for the scion of a long line of village idiots. And even then, once the village idiot's son has proved his intelligence, he is laden with scholarships and encouraged to become Prime Minister. But I am not.

AMANDA. I don't see at all what you're driving at.

PRINCE. Just this. You and I are neither of us idiots. Are we agreed on that? Nevertheless, my love story seems absolutely grotesque to you. You simply cannot imagine how I could have fallen in love with such a weird creature as Léocadia.

AMANDA. I never said 'weird'.

PRINCE. Only because you have been brought up never to speak ill of the dead. But if she had been here this evening, dressed like you, as like you in features as an identical twin, you would have been bursting with hysterical giggles all the evening at her behaviour. Isn't that so? Admit it.

AMANDA (*head bowed*). Yes, I would.

PRINCE. But since we have agreed that neither of us is an imbecile, we are going to explain ourselves to each other, once and for all. Sit down.

AMANDA. Why?

PRINCE. Because I am about to embark on an extremely long speech.

And indeed he is.

Right. Life is a wonderful thing to talk about, or to read about in history books—but it is terrible when one has to live it. It is almost impossible to sleep for more than twelve hours a day, and the remaining twelve hours have to be filled in somehow. There are, of course, the classic diversions—drink and drugs. But personally I have no taste for happiness induced by chemical compounds. There is, too, the determined brightness of the Boy Scout breed, who fill every second with some useless but efficiently performed task—but that sort of behaviour requires a special talent which, mercifully, is distributed by providence as parsimoniously as any other. As for the method which consists of leaping out of the right side of the bed every morning in the chilly dawn, and doing Swedish exercises in front of an open window, repeating incessantly that every day and in every way things are getting better and . . . (*He shudders.*) No. That's nothing but a spiritual laxative, and not for me. Consequently—I was bored. 'But you have everything in the world', they used to say to me. 'It's downright ungrateful to be bored when there's so much poverty about.' What gloriously muddled thinking! One might just as well tell a man who can't afford the price of a loaf of bread that he has no right to complain, but on the contrary, is extremely lucky, for he has good digestion and so many millionaires are dyspeptic. He'd throw you downstairs, and quite right too. It's just the same with me. Comfort can be taken for granted just as easily as a good digestion, you know. And only a fool could find happiness in comfort alone. I was bored. 'Ah,' they said, 'if you had to work eight hours a day for your living, young man—' I don't doubt it. If I had been poor and confronted daily with a factory bench or a pile of ledgers, I would have had the precious opportunity of keeping my mind occupied all the week, and only being bored on Sundays, like everybody else. But it was my fate to be condemned to endure seven Sundays every week. I really did try to fill them. But somehow I didn't seem cut out for sitting on the committees of charity balls, or presiding over the meetings of societies for the encouragement of those breeds of horses which run faster than their competitors. As for the idea of working to amass a still larger fortune, I'm sure you'll agree that would be positively immoral. What more can I say? I have no artistic talent. I have no great gift of scholarship. I have a fairly good memory, it's true, but I find it ridiculous to press it into the service of recording knowledge which would never be of the slightest use to me. No, the only thing that remains for people like me is an organized and unremitting round of amusements. We all get caught up eventually in the terrible roundabout of the fashionable seasons, and, believe me, it's a dog's life. If the professional classes put half the energy, imagination and tenacity into their businesses that the idle rich do into being bored to tears in exactly the right place on exactly the right date all over Europe, they would soon make their fortunes. I haven't even any vices. Vices are wonderfully strong, simple things. But I haven't even one.

Pause, as the awful truth of what he has said penetrates his mind.

AMANDA (*soft*). Have you finished?

PRINCE. Almost. Through the clammy mists of boredom from which I had practically abandoned hope of escaping, there flashed suddenly, like a will-o'-the-wisp, a brilliant creature, whose light and warmth dispersed the fog for three short days. A preposterous character, I grant you, followed by her retinue of greyhounds and tame serpents, a creature who awoke at dusk and went to bed at dawn, and spent the night between in meaningless chatter. An orchid-eater who lived on champagne and passion, and who died for the sake of an extravagant gesture—strangled by her own scarf. And yet, this madwoman, with all her ridiculous affectations and frivolities, was intelligent. . . .

Pause. He looks at her, insolent.

Intelligence. Another goddess of whom you may have heard. Remembering her, what do I care if the guttersnipes run after me in the street, teasing me with their cruel mimicry? They used to run after her, too. In those three days, before the mists closed in again, leaving me groping for a memory I can never quite recapture, this lovely lunatic taught me the value of so many things ... of two beautiful lips which only say 'I love you' among a thousand other things; of a cool skin which is a benison of delight to touch. (*Hard.*) And also the value of your silence, and of your simple love, so happy just to bask in the sun among the carnival litter of a picnic; and the value of our bitter joys, the joys of the rest of us, who can never share your uncomplicated happiness.

Pause.

(*A cry.*) I do not love you, mademoiselle! You are beautiful—even more beautiful than she—you are desirable, you are gay and tender and compact of all manner of delights—youth, nature, life ... and even common sense into the bargain. But I do not love you!
AMANDA (*after a tiny pause*). Have you quite finished now?
PRINCE. Yes, I have finished.
AMANDA. Well, personally, you leave me cold.

She gets up with dignity, crosses the restaurant and goes out.
The PRINCE, *having got his tirade off his chest, is very proud of himself. He looks round, and finds that he is alone. Automatically, he goes to his table and as the* HEAD WAITER *approaches, he says, pathetically*. . . .

PRINCE. *You* never doubted that I loved her more than all the world, did you, Ferdinand?
HEAD WAITER (*pouring champagne, obsequious*). Oh, sir!

How can you ask such a thing! You worshipped her. We all remarked on it, amongst ourselves. Such great love was unforgettable, sir—even to us, who only stand and wait.

As the PRINCE, *who had fallen into a reverie, puts his head in his hands, the* HEAD WAITER *turns to the orchestra, and says with an ignoble wink:*

Music!

The musicians, sniggering, strike up the waltz theme. The PRINCE *sits with his head in his hands, then wearily lays his head on the table and sleeps. The* HEAD WAITER *stops the music with a gesture. The* GIPSIES, *with audible sighs of relief, set about packing up their instruments, while the* WAITERS *clear away the tables and chairs. The* CLOAKROOM ATTENDANT *emerges from her lair carrying a selection of extremely mundane mackintoshes and caps, which the* GIPSIES *put on over their gay costumes. The* CLOAKROOM ATTENDANT *herself exchanges her perilously tottering high-heeled shoes for a pair of homely felt slippers; the* HEAD WAITER *dons a dignified overcoat and homburg hat. The glasses and bottles are stacked away. The Blue Danube has closed for the evening. Before they go, the* GIPSIES *complete the transformation scene by swinging back the hinged flats which represent the walls of the nightclub—to reveal the façade of the Chime of Bells. A table is moved here, a chair there—and before our eyes a new scene is set, representing the terrace outside the little country inn. The* GIPSIES, *their work done, pick up their instruments and depart. The* HEAD WAITER, *after a last, proprietory look round, follows them. At his table in the shadows the* PRINCE *sleeps on, his head on his arms.* AMANDA *enters from the other side of the stage. Worn out with grief and exhaustion, she sinks on to the ground, at first in tears, then in uneasy sleep. Slowly, dawn creeps into the sky—a dawn of rose-pink and grey.*

There is the sound of a shot far away. Then another, closer. The DUCHESS *and* HECTOR *appear in antiquated hunting costume, armed with shot-guns. They are followed by a* GHILLY, *who carries spare guns and empty game bags.*

GHILLY. Your shot, Lord Hector.

HECTOR *fires.*

HECTOR (*annoyed*). Missed!
GHILLY. Your shot, Your Grace.

The DUCHESS *fires.*

DUCHESS (*delighted*). Missed! I am always delighted when I miss a bird. I love to see them in flight—they are so graceful, so carefree, so confident. I can never understand why, on certain arbitrary dates, we have to start pumping lead into the poor things.

Suddenly she sees something white lying on the ground, and screams.

Heavens! What's that white thing? Did you hit something, Hector?
HECTOR. I ... I don't think so ...
GHILLY (*inspecting* AMANDA). It's the young lady who is visiting Your Grace.
DUCHESS. Oh, my God. Is she hurt?
GHILLY. No. She's asleep, Your Grace.
DUCHESS (*going to* AMANDA). Asleep, and hurt too. Her face is still covered with tears.

AMANDA *wakes, and gives a little cry when she sees the* DUCHESS.

AMANDA. Oh! Oh, it's you, madame! No, please don't speak to me.... I don't want to see anybody ... I just want to get away from here as fast as I can.

DUCHESS (*motioning the others to go*). Get away, child? Why?

AMANDA. She's too strong for me, madame.... I laugh at her, and I think I'm stronger than she is ... but I'm not. She's too strong for me....

DUCHESS. She is very strong, child, but she is no stronger than you. Remember that she has one enormous disadvantage for any young woman. She is dead.

AMANDA. She wouldn't even let him hold her hand. But his hands aren't really hard ... they are simple, strong hands, made for loving ... if only he would listen to what his hands tell him ... but he won't. So you see, I must go away, because she's stronger than I am.

DUCHESS. You are twenty years old, you are alive and in love. There is nobody in the whole world stronger than you are this morning. Look around you, instead of brooding over last night's miseries ... look. It's morning now.

And sure enough the light has brightened and the scene is transformed as the DUCHESS *speaks.*

DUCHESS. The sun is already trembling on the brink of dawn. Everything living stirs and opens at his touch, the crocuses, the young reluctant beech leaves, and the shutters of honest folk. Oh, and the smells! The first early morning smells! The smell of the earth, the smell of wet grass, and the smell of new-made coffee, which is the incense we offer at Aurora's shrine.

And indeed the LANDLORD *of the inn has opened his shutters and is already brewing coffee. Later he brings out the little trees in tubs and the tables on to the terrace.*

And look . . . you can see the first colours of the day . . . vibrant green and tender pink. Soon you will hear the buzzing of the first bee, and feel the first tingle of warmth from the sun. Léocadia may have had the witchery of the night on her side . . . but you are twenty, and alive, and in love. Look up at the sun, and laugh! All the strength of the morning is yours.

The DUCHESS *disappears, discreetly. The sun suddenly comes out with a triumphant burst of music.* AMANDA *stretches her arms and laughs up into the sunshine. The music ends with her happy laughter. She goes over to the inn, where the* LANDLORD *has just finished arranging the terrace.*

AMANDA. Landlord!

The LANDLORD *takes no notice.*

(*Louder*). Landlord!

Still no response. AMANDA *picks up a stone and beats a tattoo on a table-top. He looks at her, and then goes to see whether she has damaged the polished surface of his table, which he dusts angrily.*

AMANDA. Is this the Chime of Bells?

The LANDLORD *silently points to the inn-sign.*

AMANDA. Thank you. Are you dumb?
LANDLORD. Yes.
AMANDA (*not batting an eyelid, she smiles*). Don't you find it an awful nuisance, being dumb?
LANDLORD (*half-conquered by her smile, answers, still sulkily*). Oh, I manage.
AMANDA. Have you been dumb for a long time?

LANDLORD. Thirty-seven years.
AMANDA. Don't you do anything for it?
LANDLORD. I gargle.
AMANDA. Gargle? Do you really?
LANDLORD. No, not really. But then I'm not really dumb. My gargles are a Green Devil and a Skyrocket with every meal. Four a day. No more. I have to watch myself. My grandfather died of drink.
AMANDA. Why wouldn't you talk to me before?
LANDLORD. Can't be too careful. I didn't know you—never spoken to you before.
AMANDA. And now?
LANDLORD. Well, I've spoken to you now, haven't I? I know you.

Pause.

I sometimes take one in the morning, mind, if I'm pressed, in spite of my grandfather. Not often, but sometimes.
AMANDA. One what?
LANDLORD. Green Devil.
AMANDA. What's a Green Devil?
LANDLORD. It's a Skyrocket with a touch of bitters.
AMANDA. And what's a Skyrocket?
LANDLORD. Exactly the same as a Green Devil, but without the bitters. Shall I bring two Green Devils?
AMANDA. All right—two Green Devils. But d'you think the memory of your grandfather would prevent you from drinking mine as well? I'm not a bit thirsty this morning.
LANDLORD. Normally it would. But when a lady asks me—well, I'm prepared to stretch a point.

He goes into the inn, and returns with two glasses and a selection of bottles.

You from Dinard?

AMANDA. Yes.

LANDLORD. I suppose you wandered into the park by mistake?

AMANDA. Yes.

LANDLORD. I always get stray people in the summer who think this is a real hotel. It gives me quite a nice little bit of business on the side.

AMANDA. Isn't this a real hotel, then?

LANDLORD. Dear me, no. It's quite a story ... the owner of this estate is a prince—a real one, mind. And he's rebuilt in his park all the places he used to visit with his girl friend years ago. How's that for an eccentric, eh? They say he does it to remind himself of her ... personally I think it's all part of the council's crazy building scheme ... full of Freemasons it is ... rigged elections ... bribery, you mark my words. Still, that's none of my business. I look the other way.

AMANDA. And used they to meet each other there?

LANDLORD. Who?

AMANDA. The Prince and his girl friend?

LANDLORD. So they tell me.

AMANDA (*amazed*). What d'you mean? Can't you remember?

LANDLORD (*embarking on the second drink*). No, I can't, and I'll tell you why. When they told the proprietors of this inn they wanted to knock it down and rebuild it here, brick by brick—well, they'd been there seventeen years, see? They were planning to retire—got a little cottage by the sea. So they put me in to run the place.

AMANDA. But what happens when the Prince comes? Suppose he asks you questions?

LANDLORD. Oh, they briefed me good and proper, don't you worry. I've got it all pat—how they arrived in a taxi, the pair of them, how they ordered lemonade ... every detail, see? I couldn't tell it better if I'd been there and seen them for myself—and if ever I'm stuck, I make it up. But he never notices. Sometimes I wonder if he was there himself!

He goes back into the inn, delighted by the sensation he has caused.

AMANDA (*calling him back*). Landlord! Landlord!
LANDLORD (*reappearing in the doorway*). What is it now?
AMANDA. I like you.
LANDLORD (*suspicious*). Why?
AMANDA. You'll never know how much you've done for me.
LANDLORD. I have? (*He looks at her, on his guard.*) It was you ordered the Green Devils, you know. Three hundred francs.
AMANDA (*giving him the money*). There. And thank you very much.

At that moment, the PRINCE, *who has woken up, comes over to the inn, his collar turned up, shivering in the fresh morning air. Suddenly he sees* AMANDA.

PRINCE. Are you still here?
AMANDA. Yes, I'm still here.
PRINCE. You must forgive me for my rudeness last night.
AMANDA. Don't let's talk about it.
PRINCE (*an echo*). ... No ... don't let's talk about it. ...

He shivers.

AMANDA. You're shivering.
PRINCE. I always feel a little cold first thing in the morning.
AMANDA. Why don't you sit in the sun for a bit? It's quite warm already.

The PRINCE *moves forward, and looks at the inn.*

PRINCE. That's the inn where we went together . . . we sat inside near that little window with the red curtains. It was very cold that day.

AMANDA. We'll sit on the terrace, shall we? It's so warm this morning.

PRINCE (*coming back to earth as he bumps into a chair on the terrace*). Yes . . . forgive me . . . yes, if you like. . . . I . . . I tripped over a chair . . . clumsy of me . . . I'm afraid I'm only half awake. . . .

AMANDA. Don't you ever get up early?

PRINCE. I generally go to bed at dawn. But I'm afraid I dozed off in the nightclub . . . and now I hardly know whether I'm late to bed or early to rise.

He shivers.

How terribly cold it is.

AMANDA. Honestly, it's quite warm . . . listen to the bees . . . they wouldn't be buzzing like that if it was cold, now would they?

PRINCE (*ironic*). I suppose it's impossible for the bees to make a mistake.

He sees that AMANDA *is smiling.*

Why do you smile?

AMANDA. I thought you looked terrible last night. But you're even worse this morning.

PRINCE (*still shivering*). I do not look terrible.

The LANDLORD *comes out, surprised. He approaches the* PRINCE.

LANDLORD. Good morning, sir. Am I to serve the lemonade out here instead of indoors?

AMANDA. We don't want lemonade. Bring two cups of white coffee, good and hot. The gentleman is very cold.

LANDLORD (*thunderstruck*). White coffee! Oh, well. I only

suggested lemonade because it always has been lemonade, every day for two years. If you'd rather have coffee, you shall have coffee. It's none of my business.

AMANDA (*calling after him*). Big cups, with bread and butter!

LANDLORD (*past surprise*). Big cups . . . with bread and butter.

He goes, muttering.

Wouldn't have believed it. She's a one, she is.

AMANDA. You don't mind if we have breakfast together?

PRINCE. No, I don't mind.

He shoos away an inquisitive bee.

Another of the brutes. . . .

AMANDA. Oh, don't hurt it!

PRINCE. I suppose it would amuse you to see me eaten alive?

AMANDA. It won't eat you!

PRINCE. Are you sure?

AMANDA. Positive!

PRINCE. You seem very much at home in the morning.

AMANDA. And it's very nice to have you with me . . . allow me to introduce you, Prince Albert . . . the trees . . . the sun . . . the bees. . . .

PRINCE (*looks at her, murmuring*). You are quite terrifying.

AMANDA. Really?

PRINCE. You are like a tiny pink and white ogre.

The LANDLORD *brings out coffee in big blue cups and a plate of bread and butter.*

LANDLORD. Two white coffees. Bread and butter.

He puts them on the table.

Are you sure you wouldn't like me to bring the lemonade as well, sir?

AMANDA. No!

LANDLORD. No, she says. I don't know what the place is coming to....

> *He goes in again, grumbling. The* PRINCE *watches* AMANDA, *who is buttering a piece of bread.*

PRINCE. Do you really propose to eat all that?

AMANDA. I certainly do. And it's no good looking at me like that. I'm not ashamed of myself. I'm hungry.

PRINCE. A tiny pink and white ogre, serene and sure of herself, without a trace of tears or shame. You frighten me. Who are you?

AMANDA. Just a girl in a white dress buttering a piece of bread in the sunshine.

PRINCE. Didn't I meet you the other evening in the park beside the obelisk?

AMANDA. Yes, and I asked you the way to the sea.

PRINCE. Was that three days ago?

AMANDA. It was. The next day we met again in your aunt's house, and then we hired a boat and rowed up the river almost as far as Dinard. Then yesterday evening, after that long lazy afternoon in the sunshine, we went to the Blue Danube. You remember—the café where those ridiculous gipsies churn out mock-Viennese music....

> *She sings the refrain of the waltz. The* PRINCE *joins in softly. The orchestra takes up the theme in the background. Then* AMANDA *stops singing and the music dies.*

And now it's morning. And we are having breakfast at the Chime of Bells—the little inn you wanted to show me. Oh, it's a nice place in the morning sun!

PRINCE (*a cry*). But this is the last day!

AMANDA (*calm*). The last? What do you mean? It's the third day—and it's only just beginning.

PRINCE. But—this evening?
AMANDA. This evening? We'll go wherever you like.
PRINCE. And tomorrow morning?
AMANDA. We'll have breakfast together, just like this morning, and it will be the beginning of our fourth day.

Pause. The PRINCE *shivers—*AMANDA *takes his arm.*

You're still cold. Let's go inside.

The PRINCE *enters the inn and goes straight to a little table near the window.*

AMANDA (*stopping him quite naturally*). No, not there. That's out of the sun. This one is better.
PRINCE. No!
AMANDA. Why not? You've known me for three days, just as you knew her—and you are in love with me, just as you were with her.
PRINCE (*a cry*). I don't love you!
AMANDA (*soft*). If you didn't love me you wouldn't deny it so vehemently . . . oh, please, wake up from your horrible dream! It's morning now . . . look, the world is full of ordinary, solid, real things. Flowers you can smell and grass you can pull up and crush in your hands.

She is very close to him. Suddenly she says:

Put your two hands on my shoulders . . . you'll find everything will suddenly be so simple. . . .
PRINCE. I am afraid.
AMANDA. Touch me . . . please touch me!
PRINCE. If I touched you, Amanda, I think I would love you—but I don't want to touch you!
AMANDA (*with a little tender smile*). I'm not a bit frightened of you. Even yesterday, you seemed a very grand person, miles above me, but now you only seem like a little fish

battering his tiny fins against the whole force of the mighty river. . . .

PRINCE (*sighing, in spite of himself*). Léocadia. . . .

AMANDA (*softly*). Yes, my love. Put your hands on my shoulders. . . .

> *Pause. Suddenly the* PRINCE *puts his hands on* AMANDA'S *shoulders, and stands quite still. She closes her eyes.*

(*Whispering*). Why don't you say anything? Now *I* am afraid. . . .

PRINCE (*a strange, wondering voice*). But it is so simple . . . and so real . . . and so safe. . . .

> *Suddenly he embraces her passionately. The shutters of the little inn close tactfully on them. The* DUCHESS *and* HECTOR *come in, guns at the trail. The* GHILLY *walks behind them, carrying a bulging game bag.*

DUCHESS. It was you. I know it was you.

HECTOR. It couldn't have been me!

DUCHESS. You're such a clumsy oaf, I knew you'd have to go and kill a bird sooner or later.

HECTOR. I distinctly saw you taking aim! I'm prepared to swear it in a court of law!

DUCHESS. Really, Hector, you don't imagine I'd brief my lawyers just to make you admit you'd shot a heron.

GHILLY. It's not a heron, Your Grace—nor even a flamingo. It's an outlandish sort of bird you don't often see in these parts. Funny sort of creature. Its feathers are much too long, they get caught up in the branches when it tries to fly, and its feet are so arched it can't perch anywhere. You can see it miles away, with that tuft of bright-coloured feathers on its head . . . and as for the noise it makes . . . well, you heard that ridiculous squawk when

Your Grace fired that shot—there's no other known species makes a noise like that.

HECTOR. You see? It was you. Germain corroborates me.

DUCHESS. Very well, it was me. Now are you satisfied? (*To the* GHILLY.) We don't need you any more, Germain. You can go—and take the bird with you.

GHILLY. What shall I do with it, Your Grace? It's not even any good for eating.

DUCHESS. Bury it.

GHILLY. Very good, Your Grace.

He touches his cap, and is about to go when the DUCHESS *stops him.*

DUCHESS. Germain....

GHILLY. Your Grace?

DUCHESS (*very tender*). Bury it in my rose-garden.

The GHILLY *touches his cap, and goes. Pause.* HECTOR *and the* DUCHESS *sit on the bench side by side, pensive.*

DUCHESS (*suddenly brusque*). What are you thinking about, Hector?

HECTOR. It's funny. I was thinking about——

DUCHESS. So was I. It is funny. Poor Léocadia. She was reduced to strangling herself with her own scarf, and now we have killed her again—we have killed her memory. But Albert had to be saved. And if Amanda is the person who can save him, then good luck to her. But all the same... however useless, however frivolous and fundamentally unjust that poor, silly, orchidaceous scatterbrain may have been, surely nobody can blame us for pitying her now... and shedding a tear for her....

HECTOR (*moved*). No.... of course not....

DUCHESS (*turning on him, severe*). I was not talking to you, Hector.

81

She looks up at the sky.

I was talking to Gaston.

She gets up briskly, and goes, followed by HECTOR, *at a jog trot as*——

THE CURTAIN FALLS